Letterati

An Unauthorized Look at Scrabble®
and the People Who Play It

Paul McCarthy

ECW

Published by ECW Press
2120 Queen Street East, Suite 200, Toronto, Ontario, Canada M4E 1E2
416.694.3348 / info@ecwpress.com

LIBRARY AND ARCHIVES CANADA CATALOGUING IN PUBLICATION

McCarthy, Paul (Paul Edward), 1943–
Letterati: an unauthorized look at Scrabble® and the people
who play it / Paul McCarthy.

ISBN 978-1-55022-828-1

1. Scrabble (Game) — History. 1. Title.

GV1507.S3M33 2008   793.734   C2007-907102-3

Cover Design: David Gee
Text Design: Tania Craan
Typesetting: Gail Nina
Production: Rachel Brooks
Printing: Thomson-Shore

All photos courtesy of Ann Sanfedele, except page 179,
which is courtesy of Larry Sherman.

This book is set in Sabon and Franklin Gothic, and is printed on paper
that is 30% post-consumer waste content.

PRINTED AND BOUND IN THE UNITED STATES

ECW PRESS
ecwpress.com

Contents

Steve Alexander, Tim Anglin, Jessica Arts, Paul Avrin, John Babina, Nick Ballard, Mike Baron, Pat Barrett, Nathan Benedict, Louis Berney, Jim Bodenstedt, Tim Boggan, Marlene Boyda, David Boys, Dan Brinkley, Gary Brown, Dr. Linda Bunker, Lynne Butler, Cheryl Cadieux, Brian Cappelletto, Jean Carol, Gorton Carruth, John Chew, Pat Cole, Lee Cooper, Chris Cree, Bruce D'Ambrosio, Robin Pollock Daniel, Al Demers, Robert Denicola, Steve Dennis, Jan Dixon, Joe Edley, Paul Epstein, Shazzi Felstein, Bob Felt, Ann Ferguson, Leon Fernandez, Diane Firstman, Stephen Fisher, Shirley Fliesser, Alan Frank, Jeremy Frank, Lawren Freebody, Jim Geary, David Gibson, Daniel Goldman, Stu Goldman, Charles Goldstein, David Goodman, Bernard Gotlieb, John Green, Dr. Susan Greendorfer, Roz Grossman, Eileen Gruhn, Albert Hahn, Jonathan Hatch, Randy Hersom, Jim Homan, Barbara Horsting, Jim Houle, Don Jansen, Dennis Kaiser, Jeff Kastner, Zev Kaufman, Paula Kaufmann, Elizabeth Frost Knappman, Claudia Koczka, Jim Kramer, Jonathon Lazear, Frank Lee, Mark Lemley, Chris Lennon, Joe Leonard, Jerry Lerman, Robin Levin, Bob Lipton, Adam Logan, Robert Lowe, Glynn Lunney, Jr., Joey Mallick, Lew Martinez, Jere Mead, Karen Merrill, Mark Milan, Jim Miller, Susan Moon, Peter Morris, Gary Moss, Jim Neuberger, Rita Norr, Kathryn Northcut, Dr. Carol Oglesby, Steve Oliger, Sam Orbaum, Bill Palmer, Robert Parker, Jim Pate, Steve Pellinen, Steve Pfeiffer, Scott Pianowski, Steve Polatnick, Kenneth Port, Dan Pratt, Pat Prentice, David Prinz, Peg

Pywar, Stanley Rabinowitz, Larry Rand, M. G. Ravishandran, Janet Rice, Sherrie Saint John, Ann Sanfedele, Elliot Schiff, Bob Schoenman, Lester Schonbrun, Dean Scouloukas, Mike Senkiewicz, Luise Shafritz, Gordon Shapiro, Carol Shaver, Brian Sheppard, Joel Sherman, Glenda Short, Paul Sidorsky, Hilda Siegel, Alan Stern, David Stone, Dan Stock, Willie Swank-Pitzer, Graeme Thomas, Susi Tiekert, Ron Tiekert, Steve Tier, Siri Tillekeratne, Audrey Tumbarello, Mike Turniansky, Gene Tyszka, Barbara Van Alen, Alice Van Luenan, Carol Felstein Vignet, Joel Wapnick, Bob Watson, Al Weissman, Milt Wertheimer, Ginger White, Regina Wilhite, John Williams, Mike Willis.

Special thanks to my wife Paula who has lived through both the writing of this book and my many Scrabble ups and downs.

This is an unauthorized look at the history of competitive Scrabble in North America. It is not sponsored by, written for, or with the approval of Hasbro, Inc. In the text that follows, for ease of usage, I use the word "Scrabble." By using this word, I mean "Scrabble® Brand Crossword Game." Scrabble is the trademark of Hasbro, Inc. in North America and Mattel in other countries around the world.

From the time he was in high school Nick Ballard knew that he wanted to earn a living playing games. Today, as the number-one ranked backgammon player in the world, he does just that. Ballard's first love, though, was Scrabble. He was a top player in his twenties, edited *Medleys* (considered the best newsletter ever to grace the Scrabble world), and did much to develop the game. Yet Ballard couldn't earn a living from Scrabble, and so in 1994 he turned to backgammon. The problem for Ballard and others like him is the corporate control of Scrabble, which for the most part is a leisure time activity.

Scrabble is a trademarked game, and as such, is the property of Hasbro, Inc., the multibillion dollar toy and game manufacturer that over the years has bought up Parker Brothers, Selchow & Righter, Coleco, Milton Bradley, and others. Today it produces over 200 products and controls the board game market in North America. But that's not all. It claims the right to manufacture Scrabble exclusively, as well as to control all club and tournament activity in North America. That is, all clubs and tournaments must be sanctioned through the National Scrabble Association, a de facto arm of Hasbro.

For most Scrabble players this is not a problem. For them, Scrabble is lazy Sunday afternoons where the click and clack of tiles go hand in hand with munching goodies and arguing over the spelling of arcane words. Yet, Scrabble can be much more than that. Although unknown to most parlor players, over the past thirty years a cadre of committed Scrabblers, those I call the letterati, have worked to advance the game to rarefied levels, where tournaments are commonplace, and as one would expect, the lure of professional Scrabble sings a siren song to those who wish to hear it.

This is both the game that millions of parlor players know and something else all together. It does use the standard board layout and distribution of tiles that are available in any game shop, but that's where the similarity ends. The letterati have refined Scrabble to the point that the strategy and tactics used, as well as the words played, bear little resemblance to parlor play. New Scrabble club members, for instance, often only half jokingly ask when glancing at a game in progress, "Are you playing in a foreign language?" Well, no, but it can appear that way.

Even so, Scrabble remains a product and an entry in Hasbro's balance sheet. No matter how much the players have done to advance the game, they really have no say in where Scrabble is going, because it's not in the public domain like chess, checkers, or bridge. Rather, it's a trademarked good with various associated copyrights. This is fine for Snakes and Ladders or Clue, but problematic for Scrabble, which has a dedicated player base, some of whom would like to earn a living from the game. Unfortunately, from the perspective of the letterati, the owners have always asserted that they enjoy total control over Scrabble and seem to want to use it solely as a public relations vehicle to sell more Scrabble sets. Any advancement of the game would appear to be an unintended consequence. So while some of the letterati want to take Scrabble to the professional level, they have been thwarted by the trademark holders at every turn. This book tells that story at the same time as it looks at the evolution of the game and the people who play it.

For most parlor players Scrabble is just a fun, family pastime. That's the way it's sold and that's the way it's played. I first learned of another side of the game, a parallel universe if you will, some ten years ago when I joined the newly formed Honolulu club. My involvement with Scrabble, along with my commitment to learning its finer points, increased when a year later I moved to Colorado and became a member of the Denver club.

I discovered that I was a babe in the Scrabble woods. Just about everyone in the club had played longer, knew more words and strategy, and had more natural ability. There were methods of studying and techniques of playing that I had never dreamt of. There were also those who committed large chunks of their lives to mastering this ever fascinating and often frustrating game. This book provides a glimpse of that world. It focuses on the ways in which the players have developed the game, how they play the game, what it takes to excel, and how the game's owners have actually stood in the way of this development.

The story begins three decades ago in New York's public game rooms, where many of the conventions of contemporary tournament play were born. It goes on to explore the foundations of organized play that came along in the 1970s and '80s; the first clubs and tournaments instituted by Selchow & Righter, the game's manufacturer at the time; the compilation of the *Official Scrabble Players Dictionary*; the development of the North American rating system; and the formation of the players' organizations, run for the benefit of the game's owners. Most importantly, it tells the story of the players, who through their own efforts have made the clubs and tournaments work and the game advance from a fun, family activity to the full contact, brain bending, mind sport that at its topmost levels it is today.

Letterati also looks at how the clubs and tournaments are run and why so few people, out of the tens of millions who play at home, ever get involved in the organized game. It also shows how the letterati learn all those words and the lengths to which some go to compete, including playing hurt and cheating. There are also chapters that tease out the qualities exhibited by the top players, show how the game has changed over the years, explore the reasons for the lack of top women players, and profile teen prodigies.

Throughout the book there is a concern, shared by many players, about the control exercised by Hasbro, Inc. The players are not allowed to earn a living from the game, solicit outside sponsorship for their tournaments, or, for all practical purposes, write how-to books. There would appear to be something inherently unfair about this, even if Hasbro does own the rights to the game. These issues are addressed in the hope that one day the players and the company will be able to reach some sort of accommodation that will allow Scrabble to flower.

The original owners of Scrabble, Alfred Butts and James Brunot, sold the North American rights to the game to Selchow & Righter in 1971. Coleco Industries bought S&R and owned the game from 1986–89. Then the multibillion dollar Hasbro, with its subsidiary Milton Bradley, bought the game in 1989 and has owned it ever since. They have kept Scrabble on a short leash. I got a sense of this six years ago when I helped organize my first tournament. I had been delegated some tasks by the Denver club director, Laura Scheimberg. Among other things, to call the

National Scrabble Association to obtain mailing labels, so that we could send out event announcements to other clubs. As soon as I opened my mouth, an interrogation began, "Who are you? Are you an NSA member? A tournament director?" and so on. There was an obvious tone of skepticism in the voice on the other end of the line. There was no mistake about it. This was a policing function.

Despite their commitment to the game, the players have never had a special relationship with the game's owners. For the companies it has just been business. The trademark holders have put in place various policies backed by dubious legal claims, which ensure that the competitive game has no chance to reach its potential. For the most part, this means it is not allowed to expand beyond small tournaments controlled by the company. This approach to the game is justified by the company as a means of protecting its trademark.

In spite of this oppressive atmosphere, a dedicated group of tournament players exists. Many of these letterati are oblivious to the politics of the game, some resent their corporate master, and still others seem to lead double lives. They recognize what Hasbro is doing, but their commitment to the game means that they continue to play, accepting paltry, periodic handouts from their sometimes patron, in exchange for grudging fealty.

The book reflects this love/hate relationship. I have been swept up by the game. I've invested thousands of hours over the past decade learning to play. I've spent thousands of dollars to attend tournaments and committed countless hours to putting on our Denver event. I respect the time, effort, and money that players devote to this passion.

Tournament and club players, though, are essentially workers on the trademark holder's PR plantation. They show the Scrabble flag and spread the Scrabble word through the 200-plus Scrabble clubs that exist in North America and the hundreds of tournaments that club members put on each year. In return, the players are allowed to pay (they must be NSA members) to participate in these tournaments, which are loosely sanctioned by the National Scrabble Association, a quasi PR arm of Hasbro. Some players wait for the big money events that seldom happen, while others are just happy to be able to play the game. For those who would like to see organized Scrabble develop into something more than podunk tournaments in which the players themselves ante up the prize money, this stunted form of the game is not enough.

Whether tournament Scrabble at the highest level could ever grasp the public imagination, or at least a sliver of it, and support a professional tier of players is debatable. A handful of unauthorized events already exist in Southeast Asia, where the trademark holder has no sway. Some people feel the game may blossom there. The World English Language Scrabble Players Association (WESPA) is also in embryonic form. It has support from over twenty countries (the U.S. is notably absent) and the promise of big-time events is in the offing. What appears certain is that the way Scrabble is organized now, it is unlikely to flower in North America, the place where it was invented. The pages that follow reveal both faces of this exciting game—the players and the owners. With any luck they'll find a way to bridge the divide that separates them. At any rate, let's hope so.

I

The New York Game Rooms

1960s Hustlers Refine the Game

Alfred Butts, an unemployed architect, developed Scrabble while living in Jackson Heights, New York, in the 1930s, but it wasn't marketed under its present name, board configuration, and tile distribution until 1948. The game sold with little fanfare and in small numbers for close to five years. Then, in 1953, Scrabble exploded into the public consciousness as sales went through the roof. It isn't totally clear why. Some say it was due to its sale through Macy's department store in New York and the associated publicity that this engendered. Others felt the boom resulted from the steady, but limited, sales of the game producing a critical mass of players. Whatever the reasons, it remained just a game for the next fifteen years. It wasn't until the 1960s that the modern strategy and tactics of serious Scrabble slowly emerged.

When Selchow & Righter (s&R) instituted organized

Alfred Butts (L), Scrabble inventor, made an appearance at a
tournament at Arby's in New York City in 1981, seen here
with Dave Schulman.

Scrabble with clubs and tournaments in the early 1970s,
even though there were good players in San Francisco,
Chicago, and Toronto, it was generally recognized that the
top tile pushers were in New York City. There was a
reason for that. They developed in the public game rooms,
places like the Fleahouse and the Chess House in the
1960s, and Chess City, the Game Room, and to a lesser
extent the Bar Point Club and the Olive Tree, a Greenwich
Village coffee house, in the late 1970s and early 1980s. It
was a phenomenon unique to New York.

The New York game rooms were places where the
public could play chess, checkers, backgammon, poker,
gin rummy, and sometimes bridge, depending on the time
and place. The equipment was rented and the players paid

by the hour, says Les Schonbrun, of Oakland, California, who cut his Scrabble teeth at the Fleahouse in the mid 1960s and is the only competitor from that era still active in tournament play. Located on 42nd Street near Broadway, the Fleahouse, also known as the New York Chess and Checkers Club, was where serious Scrabble, not unlike what exists at the tournament level today, was born. A few men, and fewer women, gathered to match wits for a penny or two a point and refine the rules of what for most Americans was a family game.

Except for the nights when Fran Goldfarb played, there wasn't much to look at at the Fleahouse, according to Jeff Kastner, an Arizona marketing executive, who began playing there in 1969. The Fleahouse was owned by John Fursa, a gruff and scruffy looking fellow, who usually locked the doors after midnight and wouldn't let you in unless he knew you, says Schonbrun. And for good reason. The area was also home to numerous porn theaters, sex shops, and various unsavory characters.

You had to walk up a long set of creaky stairs, says Kastner. The place always smelled. "It's hard to describe, but somewhere between a men's locker room and a cheap bar," he says. It was not uncommon for the occasional derelict to wander in. "The tables, chairs, and walls had the look of a rundown school cafeteria," says Kastner, but there were large windows that offered a view of 42nd Street, such as it was. The chess, checkers, backgammon, and Scrabble sets were old and in need of replacement. Fist fights and cursing in various languages were acceptable behavior. "The bathrooms stank of urine and semen," says Kastner. "Need I say more?" Schonbrun remembers it was mostly frequented by hustlers and Eastern European emigrés. Two or three players were explosively violent and you had to be careful around them, he says. "There was a guy named Sal, with a Neanderthal jaw and brow, who was brutishly strong, not a bad chess and Scrabble player, but who shook people down when he was low on funds."

Charles Goldstein, who now lives in Berkeley, California, has similar recollections. Goldstein first went there to play chess when he was still a high school student in the 1960s. Later, while at Brooklyn College, he would drop in to play Scrabble. He didn't play the top people, who he remembers as "old guys who were not very friendly and smoked a lot," although Richie Gilston, an editor at Funk & Wagnalls, did clobber him once. His most vivid memory, though, is of literally being clobbered. "I beat this guy pretty badly," says Goldstein, who would go on to finish fifth in the 1978 North American Invitational, "so he flipped over the board and then punched me in the eye."

Still, this was the place where it started. Schonbrun first went to the Fleahouse with some physics graduate students who liked to play chess. It wasn't long before he discovered his gift for Scrabble. While he was recovering from his first marriage, a friend, Al Tesoro, was avoiding his physics dissertation. They got into sessions that lasted for days. "We didn't take breaks," says Schonbrun, "just had soup and sandwiches over the board, watched the day players come in and leave, come in and leave again."

People like Charlie Hendricks, Paul Brandts, Asa Hoffman, Shelby Lyman, and Richie Gilston played too. And, of course, there was Bernie Wishengrad, who would later win the New York City Championship twice, and Mike Senkiewicz, whom S&R would tap in 1972 to set up tournament Scrabble pretty much as it is today. They played with chess clocks (eighteen minutes for the score-keeper, fifteen for his opponent), the double challenge rule (gain a turn if you're right, lose one if you're wrong) and the *Funk & Wagnalls College Dictionary.*

They also played for money. Against one another it was mostly for practice, bragging rights, and to make things interesting, says Kastner. But when they "hustled fish," people from off the street, they gave handicaps such as money, time odds, free challenges, or spotted points (instead of starting from zero the opponent was given some arbitrary number of points, say 100, before the game began). The idea was to fleece the unsuspecting. Some of these guys were Runyonesque characters, according to Kastner. Hoffman was a chess master who could hustle almost any board or card game, including Scrabble. A good part of the time he slept on chairs in the backroom and spent his days at the track. "He was so notorious," says Kastner, "he was featured in the chess film *Searching for Bobby Fischer.*"

Shelby Lyman was another chess whiz, who hosted the TV coverage of the 1972 Fischer-Spassky World Championship. Bernie Wishengrad was a great handicapper who made his living at the track, while Richie Gilston was a writer/editor, who never had the nerves for tournament Scrabble but was a fine player in his own right. Brandts was also a chess master who often played Scrabble against Schonbrun and Mike Senkiewicz, considered the top two players in New York City. "I learned a lot from kibbitzing those sessions," says Kastner.

There were also a few women players, but they were scarce at the Fleahouse, where the price of admission was an obsession with the game and a willingness to negotiate the neighborhood. Kastner recalls Shazzi Felstein, who placed ninth at the 1978 North American Invitational, Fran Goldfarb, and a "Scrabble Rosie." The sleaziness was a big deterrent to women, says Schonbrun. "Everyone was smoking and sallow-faced," he says. "There was nothing to attract anyone who wasn't totally absorbed with chess, Scrabble, or bridge."

Kastner remembers his first visit to the Fleahouse well. He was a student at NYU at the time and captain of the chess team. It didn't take long for Asa Hoffmann, a chess master, to sidle over and ask if he wanted to play. Naturally, they played for the time and equipment rental. Hoffmann wore army fatigues and pretended to be on leave. A likely fish. "He even had me explain to him how to use the chess lock," says Kastner, who partway into the game realized he was being conned.

The approach to hustling Scrabble fish was similar, according to Kastner. They had to believe that they could beat you, he says, "so you had to play just good enough to win." That meant not playing words that would frighten them away or winning by too much, something that was easier to do in chess, which is mostly skill, than in Scrabble, which also involves the luck of the draw. Kastner found that as he played more, and became a regular, that his reputation preceded him. "So I often had to spot enormous odds of money, time, or points to lure the fish into playing me," he says.

Numerous present-day Scrabble conventions were born at the Fleahouse, but there were also some differences with today's play. As previously mentioned, the time allotment was one of them, with eighteen minutes for the score-keeper and fifteen for his opponent, considerably shorter than the twenty-five minutes allowed each player today. Both parties tally the score today, which cuts down on errors. Still, Schonbrun says that people played sessions back then—anywhere from four to twelve games with the same person, at say two cents a point, so it was the total point spread that people cared about. They alternated keeping score and assumed the errors would average out over the long haul.

The "look-up" rule was different too. It was "you played it, you find it," rather than using an impartial person to look up the word. This flies in the face of the common-sense feeling today that no one wants to give an opponent the opportunity to scan the dictionary and learn the correct spelling of a word, or possibly discover a whole new word that can be formed from the same letters. It made a degree of sense, though, when using the *Funk & Wagnalls Dictionary*, because for many words, a player had to know where to look. Who would know better, for example, that MARIA (the plural of MARE) was found under MARE, than the person who played it.

The practice can be defended on other grounds. Schonbrun still feels that the possibility that a player might have found something useful was outweighed by the fact that he had only himself to blame if he looked up the word incorrectly and couldn't find it. Steve Polatnick, a Miami lawyer, who began playing at the Game Room in 1978, liked the rule too, and still uses it with friends. He recalls, though, how it was once used against him.

He was new to serious Scrabble and was up against Gary Fredericks, who lay down OUTROPE. Polatnick challenged the play, and Fredericks looked it up. At first he seemed dejected, then "his eyes lit up," according to Polatnick. Fredericks said OUTROPE was no good, gave up his turn, watched Polatnick play, and then threw down OUT-PORE. "I figured," says Polatnick, "that while looking up OUTROPE he had found OUTPORE, which isn't good either. He gave a brilliant performance and fooled me." Despite being outsmarted, Polatnick recounts the tale with an obvious trace of admiration for Fredericks, even a quarter century after the fact. It was a different time and place, which rewarded a different style of play than today.

Ron Tiekert, one of Scrabble's all-time greats, recalls how he took advantage of the look-up rule when playing the formidable Jim Neuberger at the Game Room. *Funk & Wagnalls* was famous for its lists. OVER- and -OUT words, among others, were in lists under OVER and OUT, but some lists were less obvious. Neuberger had played DIEMAKER, a nice find, but Tiekert suspected that Neuberger would look under D if he were challenged and not under M where the MAKER list resided. And he was right. Tiekert challenged and won when Neuberger couldn't find the acceptable DIEMAKER. "To some extent it was a guilty pleasure," says Tiekert, "but ethical in the context of the game rooms."

There were other differences with play in the '60s and today's play. Tiles were drawn from a shallow box, where they rested face down. Another chance for the hustler to get one up. Les Schonbrun says he had been around for a while, was already one of the best players in the club, but one day discovered he wasn't privy to the blank scam. He had just won a session against a seasoned player who stalked off saying, "You're the luckiest fish on earth." Schonbrun was puzzled and asked another regular what the guy was talking about. This regular picked out the blanks, which were face down in the box. "I guess he thought he could beat you if

Ron Tiekert at the North American Invitational in 1983.

he got all the blanks," he told an astonished Schonbrun.

The blanks were a cinch to spot, according to Schonbrun, if you knew what to look for. The tiles were made of a light-colored wood, but the blanks were always a little lighter. The blanks rested on each of their sides about half the time, so they got half as dirty as the other tiles, which were always face down. At one point the "split blank rule" solved the problem. At the beginning of the game each player was given a blank to use when he saw fit. Schonbrun recalls that it did solve the problem, but "that no one loved it that much, either." When tile bags came in, the split blank rule went out, and many of the players were glad to see it go, he says.

A further variance with today's play was board orientation. It's inconceivable to most players now, but in the 1960s and through much of the 1970s, serious Scrabble was played on cheap cardboard sets, not the lazy-Susan type boards with nonslip, indented cells for the tiles, that everyone uses today. To avoid jostling the letters out of position, the boards were never turned. Instead, the players sat across from one another, with the board at right angles, so each could read the tiles equally well. Ron Tiekert, who began playing at the Chess House in 1971, says he played his first 5000 games that way.

Tiekert only played at the Fleahouse a few times, but recalls another difference between play then and contemporary play. There was no tile tracking—the tallying of tiles as they are used, so a player knows which tiles remain. "They might count out the tiles at the end of a game, time permitting," says Tiekert, but they neither constructed a tracking sheet during the game nor used the preprinted tracking sheets (which list all the tiles) that are favored today. Early players also tended to emphasize "tile turnover," playing as many tiles as possible, to increase the chances of drawing the blanks (the most valuable tiles), an approach that is no longer considered good strategy.

Another place where a lot of Scrabble was played was the Chess House, located in a spacious townhouse on

72nd Street between Broadway and Columbus Avenue, says Kastner. The first floor accommodated about forty people, who paid a dollar and a quarter an hour to play Scrabble, chess, checkers, backgammon, Go, and other board games. Kastner recalls a backroom for contract bridge, a full kitchen, and a room on the second floor for poker, gin rummy, and table tennis. In 1976, when he took over from Mike Senkiewicz as manager of the Manhattan Chess Club, Kastner got very cozy with the Chess House. "It was my main haunt," he says, "especially after I moved to the neighborhood. I was there from about six p.m. to the wee hours most nights." It was owned by Charlie Hidalgo, a strong chess player. Some of the people who played there were Frank Kuehnrich, Joe Richman, Steve Brandwein, Linda Gruber, the late Steve Pfeiffer, and beginning in 1971, a green but eager Ron Tiekert.

It was at the Chess House in 1974 or 1975 that Gary Brown witnessed the famous OUISTITI match between Schonbrun and Senkiewicz. "They were like gods to serious players," says Brown. Schonbrun was visiting from Oakland, California, where he had resided since 1970. On this particular night he was losing badly. He was drawing poorly and Senkiewicz had just plopped down CLARETS. The game looked like a drubbing, according to Brown. The s of CLARETS, though, sat on the fourth square over from the left on the bottom row, setting up a triple/triple possibility, the highest scoring play in Scrabble. But Schonbrun had IIIOTTU. He took a lot of time with it, says Brown. "We were all looking, at each other thinking, 'What's he doing? He's got nothing.'" Then Schonbrun slapped down OUISTITI (a South American monkey) for 122 points. "It was the only time I've seen people applaud," says Brown. Now players study eight-letter bingos (a word of seven or more letters) regularly and OUISTITI, while a good find, would not be that surprising, "but back then," says Brown, "it was just amazing."

As the popularity of chess waned, the Chess House became the House of Games and eventually folded in 1976 or 1977. It was replaced by a club that popped up in 1973 called Chess City, located at 100th Street and Broadway. Jim Neuberger played Scrabble there, along with Steve Williams, Bob Richardson, Ann Sanfedele, Paul Avrin, Stu Goldman, Steve Pfeiffer, and Rick Rutman, among others. Neuberger recalls playing there on the night of the blackout of 1977. "We all continued playing by candlelight," he says, "while we could hear crowds looting in a store below. It was pretty scary."

Many of the top players got their starts at Chess City, says Brown. He gives the credit to the late Mike Martin, who worked there. To conjure up Martin, says Brown, just think of Dustin Hoffman playing Ratso Rizzo in *Midnight Cowboy*. "The gray suit, the expressions, the vocabulary, the mannerisms. That was Mike Martin," says Brown. He had an uncanny ability to gauge how much stronger he was than a new player and would offer just the right spot, say fifty points, to make the game interesting. And since they were playing for a penny a point, says Brown, "It was good, because you could learn a lot without the fear of losing a lot." As the newcomer improved, Martin would decrease the spot. Ron Tiekert and Steve Pfeiffer started that way, says Brown.

Brown himself helped some players to develop. The chess-club players were much better than those who competed in the early Scrabble clubs sponsored by S&R. After

Brown started his Brooklyn club in 1975, he tried to groom members for the stiffer competition they would face in the city. When he thought someone was ready, he would take them to the game rooms in Manhattan. "I felt I helped some players improve a lot," he says.

After several location changes the Chess House became the Game Room and in 1978 settled into quarters in the basement of the Beacon Hotel at 75th Street and Broadway. According to Kastner, as you walked down the stairs you came "face-to-face with a graffiti mural depicting games." There was a dimly lit bar on the left, video games and a TV where most of the Chess City regulars continued to play and were augmented by Carol Clarke, Sharon Swerdloff and sometimes Ed Halper, Steve Alexander, and Steve Polatnick. The club was owned by Stuart Morden and Jerry Bernstein, who had owned Chess City. It was presided over by Mike Martin, while Ron Tiekert, now an accomplished player, functioned as the in-house expert. It was open twenty-four hours a day.

For a dollar and a quarter an hour there was Scrabble, Boggle, backgammon, chess, checkers, or gin rummy. For a while a sanctioned Scrabble club even met there, run by Mike Martin, who bestowed nicknames on all the regulars. Stu Goldman was Goo Stolman, Tiekert was the Head Brillo, Rick Rutman was Racky Rookie, Ann Sanfedele was Fansy Deli, and Mike was the Head Prazy, to name a few. Like Kastner, Tiekert lived in the neighborhood, a three-minute walk from the Game Room. As the "house expert" he didn't have to pay "table time" and in return answered the questions of newcomers, made rulings, ran eight tournaments between 1979 and 1984, and sometimes worked behind the desk.

Tiekert got his start at the Chess House in 1971. Like so many others he had played Scrabble prior to that, but never took it seriously. Then he started to play casually on his lunch hours with fellow book editors. This led him to requisition a *Funk & Wagnalls* for his editing duties, and he began to learn the three-letter words. It wasn't long before he became a regular at the Chess House, where he discovered there was much more to Scrabble than he had thought. He got pointers from Jeff Kastner and Frank Kuehnrich and when his editing job dropped to thirty hours a week, he put in more time over the board.

Tiekert says he played well over twenty games a week from 1976 to 1979, and sometimes as many as fifty. He seldom played for more than two cents a point and a dollar a game, but says, "I netted about forty dollars a week playing Scrabble during that period." That's probably as close as anyone has come to playing for a living. Even so, Tiekert never saw himself as a hustler. He'd fess up to his skills against strangers and offer a spot, he says.

The late 1970s and early 1980s were exciting times at the Game Room. It was a mecca for serious Scrabble at a time when the clubs sponsored by Selchow & Righter were just getting off the ground and tournaments were few and far between. Steve Polatnick, for instance, would periodically come up from Miami to visit his parents on Long Island and invariably make his way to the basement of the Beacon Hotel. Polatnick was not new to the game. He had played in the Miami Scrabble club since 1974 and in the 1978 North American Invitational, so he had a bit of a reputation, but he wasn't quite ready for prime time at the Game Room. "I wasn't a total fish," he says, "but they beat me for money." It was understood, says

Polatnick, that that was the price you paid to experience high level Scrabble.

All the best players hung out at the Game Room, according to Polatnick. "It was a wild feeling to play there." The top players were called sharks. "They were dangerous and could take a lot of money from people even at two cents a point," he says. How good were they? Polatnick recalls a night when Tiekert was playing Nick Ballard, then of Chicago. A crowd had gathered as Ballard wrestled with the nice rack of AEERNST (EASTERN, EARNEST, NEAREST), and seemingly no place to play it. According to Polatnick, the onlookers sort of felt sorry for Ballard. There was the word PI in the middle of the board, though, and the assembled players' jaws dropped as Ballard plunked down PISTAREEN. Tiekert challenged, it was good, "and the crowd cheered," says Polatnick.

He also vividly remembers the first time he tangled with Tiekert. Tiekert opened with PLAIDED. The word didn't make sense to Polatnick, so he challenged. It was good. Loss of turn. Then Tiekert played LIEGEMAN through the E in PLAIDED. Polatnick incorrectly challenged that too. Loss of another turn. Not long afterward, Tiekert again threw down a seven, hooking an N to ROPE to make ROPEN, a phony. The intimidated Polatnick let it go. "The next thing I knew," he says, "I was 250 or 300 points down. At two cents a point that adds up."

Polatnick, who finished fourth in the 2001 World Championship, remembers all-night sessions when the time would slip away as they played in the underground and windowless Game Room. "You didn't know if it was day or night," he says. Polatnick often played twelve-game sessions with only a few seconds between each match.

"When the game ended the board was flipped over into a box," he says, "and the tiles were ready to go again. It was an instant recycle." By the second or third game he felt his mind was at peak efficiency. "You would get into a groove and hit the max cruising speed of your mental powers," he says. This is unlike today's tournaments, with breaks between games and changes in opponents, with ample opportunity for lapses in concentration. "The intensity was incredible," says a still-awed Polatnick. "You were mentally wrestling with your opponent."

Playing for money was, and remains to this day, an important part of the game for many of the early players. It's not the amount of money that changes hands, but playing for money focuses the mind in ways a bragging-rights match doesn't. Schonbrun recalls that when he moved to California in 1970 he discovered it was politically incorrect to play Scrabble for money. His interest waned and he dropped out of the scene for a number of years. Steve Pfeiffer, who began playing at the Chess House in 1974 and then became a Game Room regular, put it this way: "You do things when you play for fun, that you would never do when you play for money. I even play my wife for money."

Most of the Game Room players did not play in clubs sanctioned by S&R, and in fact looked down on the club players as amateurish, says Stu Goldman. Pfeiffer told a story that illustrates the gap between what was going on in the New York clubs and at kitchen tables around America. He gambled, bowled, and went to the track with a buddy who didn't play Scrabble, but whose mother did. The mother was a great player, said the buddy, who was always bugging Pfeiffer to play her. "Finally he got me pissed off

It was smoking as usual at the finals of the New York City
tournament in 1978, a few months before the first North
American Invitational. From left to right, Roz Grossman,
Steve Pfeiffer, Bernie Wishengrad, and Arnie Alpert.

one night and I said okay," recounted Pfeiffer. The friend
bet a hundred dollars a game on his mother. "We played
five games," said Pfeiffer, "and she got destroyed." Some of
the games were so one-sided that they weren't even finished. "I felt bad," he said, "but beat the guy for $500."

Pfeiffer began playing in Brooklyn, where Gary Brown
helped him hone his skills. Brown eventually brought him
to Manhattan where Pfeiffer still had to pay for his lessons, just like Polatnick and many others. "It would cost
you money to play those guys," said Pfeiffer, "that's the
way you learned words and strategy back then." First he
was spotted time. He would get fifteen minutes to play his
game, while his opponents would get seven or eight. As he

improved the spots decreased and then vanished. "You learned to play fast that way," he said.

He didn't go out of his way to hustle. In fact, he preferred to go up against the top players, so he could learn. But sometimes fish sought him out and since he didn't need the money he offered them good spots. On occasion he gave them fifteen minutes and started his own clock on zero, which meant he was over the time limit as soon as his clock was struck and lost ten points for each subsequent minute. "They thought it was a game they couldn't lose," recalled Pfeiffer, "but they learned otherwise." Pfeiffer did most of his thinking on their time.

Word of the Game Room spread and players from all over the country would drop in when they were in New York to test their skills. In 1978 Tiekert would run the first of eight Game Room tournaments, which drew between forty-eight and sixty-four entrants, depending on the event, and rewarded the top player with around $200. The events lured Joel Wapnick and Stephen Fisher from Canada, Nick Ballard from Chicago, Polatnick from Miami, and Ken Lambe from Flint, Michigan, to name a few. Jim Pate of Birmingham, Alabama, came up for three Game Room events over the years and says, "at the time they were the biggest and had the toughest competition." Winning one of Tiekert's tournaments in December of 1980 was the highlight of Stu Goldman's thirty years of tournament Scrabble. "It was even better than being sixth in the 1992 Nationals," says Goldman.

But the end of an era came in 1985 when the Game Room closed, a victim of skyrocketing commercial rents. John Fursa had already sold the Fleahouse in 1980. After that the atmosphere changed and it was no longer a haven

Stu Goldman at the NYC semi-finals at the Brooklyn War
Memorial in 1975.

for Scrabble players, says Kastner. The Chess House had
closed its doors even earlier in 1976, according to Tiekert.
And the Bar Point Club, which was never a true Scrabble
haunt, but did have a Scrabble club that was attended by
some of the better players, had closed in 1983. In just a
decade the world of non-membership hangouts for game
players changed dramatically. There were some other
clubs, but nothing ever took the place of the Game Room,
says Jim Neuberger, who played there from its first incar-
nation as Chess City. After it closed he tried some other
places, but says, "I went to them with decreasing frequency and eventually stopped all together." The heyday
of the game clubs was over.

Still, Mike Martin, who ran the Game Room, managed
to keep high-level Scrabble alive in New York. In 1985 he

started Club No.56, sanctioned by s&r. It had an average turnout of around forty, says Tiekert. The club kicked around for a few years before settling in at the Beverly Bridge Club at 57th Street and Lexington Avenue, where Martin directed from 1987 to 1998. He passed away in January 2002, a loss felt by all who knew him as the Head Prazy.

2

The Business of Scrabble

Selchow & Righter Launches the Game

In 1971, Selchow & Righter (S&R), the company that had been manufacturing Scrabble sets since 1954 under a license from James Brunot, an associate of Alfred Butts, the game's inventor, purchased Scrabble and the right to sell it in North America. The following year, to increase publicity for the game and to protect its trademark, the company decided to sponsor a nationwide network of clubs and tournaments. Jim Houle, who played a central role in this undertaking, remembers it this way.

Houle was hired in 1971 as a production supervisor at S&R's factory in Holbrook, New York. He would later head Scrabble Crossword Game Players, Inc. (SCGP), the predecessor to the National Scrabble Association (NSA). It was an arm of S&R and was set up to run Scrabble tournaments and charter clubs. Scrabble Crossword Game Players, Inc. was billed as a players' organization, but just like its successor the NSA, it was an owner's organization, with goals that were separate from any objectives the players might have had for the game. When there were conflicts between what was good for the game and best for the company, the latter always won out.

Scrabble Crossword Game Players, Inc. was formed as a corporate arm of S&R in late 1972. Through its first leader, Lee Tiffany, SCGP laid the foundation for the organized game. To the players of the time, Tiffany was a strange choice for the job, according to Jonathan Hatch, who won the inaugural Brooklyn tournament in 1973 and went on to work with Tiffany on various Scrabble promotions. "He used to brag that he had never played the game," says Hatch, whom Tiffany called "champy" because of his Brooklyn win. A still slightly miffed Hatch further recalls that Tiffany promised him and his future wife Kathy Flaherty that they would receive credit in the *Official Scrabble Players Dictionary* for the two years they spent helping to compile it, but that never materialized. "He was just an advertising kind of guy," says Hatch.

Gary Brown doesn't remember Tiffany that fondly, either. Brown got the Scrabble bug while stationed in the United Kingdom in 1970. When he came home to New York, he entered the second Brooklyn tournament in the fall of 1974. A year later he started Club No. 13 in Brooklyn. According to Brown, players of the day felt that Tiffany wasn't doing enough to get the club scene moving. Many believed it was because Tiffany didn't know anything about the game, says Brown. In response to that criticism, he says, Tiffany became known in game circles for saying, "I don't need to know anything about Kotex in order to sell it." Many players might have been just as surprised as Hatch and Brown by the kind of person s&r chose to head up scgp, but not Jim Houle, who was the third leader of that organization. "scgp was created to sell games and protect the trademark," says Houle. Tiffany was an s&r vice president for advertising. So choosing him made all the sense in the world.

Tiffany published the initial *Scrabble Players Newspaper* (*SPN*) in the spring of 1973, not long after the first Brooklyn tournament. Dan Pratt, a Baltimore player, remembers it well because that issue was distributed at the first Baltimore tournament, which was sponsored by the Baltimore Bureau of Recreation, *The Baltimore Sun*, and scgp. From the beginning, s&r made it clear that the goals of scgp were to charter and assist new Scrabble clubs, create and maintain a rating sytem, develop equipment, formulate rules, and hold tournaments. There was no mention of developing the game.

For five dollars, players could become members. For their money they got a quarterly newsletter and the *Scrabble Players Handbook*, which was full of tips and strategy. Tiffany established *Funk & Wagnalls Standard College Dictionary* as the official word source. He introduced the company's resident Scrabble expert, Mike Senkiewicz, who would write a column for *SPN* and had already done a great deal to put in place the foundation for tournament Scrabble with his work on the first Brooklyn event.

According to Senkiewicz, who hasn't played serious Scrabble for twenty years, but now plays backgammon for a living, he was brought in about a year earlier when s&r decided it wanted to start up clubs and tournaments. This was a tight knit group. Senkiewicz's girlfriend was Shazzi

Mike Senkiewicz at the New York City finals in 1978.

Felstein. She, in turn, was Joel Skolnick's sister-in-law. Skolnick worked for the Brooklyn Department of Parks and Recreation putting on community events. He got together with S&R to put on the Brooklyn tournament and recommended Senkiewicz to organize the Scrabble side of it. For s&r it was an opportunity to see if the public would turn out for Scrabble tournaments.

The Brooklyn event was held at the Brooklyn War Memorial in the fall of 1973, says Carol Felstein Vignet, who was a word judge, and at the time married to Joel Skolnick. It attracted some 500 players. Vignet feels that all s&r did "was take over an existing structure." This was because Senkiewicz, Ron Tiekert, and other New York players had advised Skolnick on how to set up the tournament using word judges, *Funk & Wagnalls*, sand timers, and various other tournament protocols, most of which were already in use in the New York City game rooms. "s&r was handed a piece of cake," says Vignet, "that turned out to be marvelous publicity that promoted Scrabble nationwide, when it had only been played seriously by a small group of eggheads."

Senkiewicz was one of those eggheads. Today he says that s&r had no idea of where to begin with tournament Scrabble, but for him "there wasn't much to create because tournament-like Scrabble was already being played in the New York chess clubs. I just had to give a formality to it," he says.

Lee Tiffany didn't take all of Senkiewicz's suggestions, which irks him to this day. Tiffany and others at s&r, according to Senkiewicz, knew nothing about gaming, while he was a professional. Still, they used what they liked and discarded what they didn't. "It was like the inventor of the automobile telling a race car driver how the car should be handled at high speeds," says Senkiewicz.

The thirty-minute game, fifteen minutes per side, the way it was played in the chess clubs, was abandoned. If adopted by s&R it would probably have intimidated the average parlor player. So s&R instituted sixty-minute games, which Senkiewicz thought made Scrabble less exciting. s&R didn't take a liking to chess clocks, either, but instead settled for the cheaper, more available, and notoriously unreliable three-minute sand timers. No doubt this was also done to make the game more affordable to the parlor player, who was unlikely to splurge on a forty-dollar clock.

There were unofficial Scrabble clubs in some cities prior to 1973, but these clubs were frowned upon by s&R. So in 1973 Tiffany announced in the second issue of the *SPN* that a director's manual was available and that scGP was ready to license official clubs. Scrabble Crossword Game Players, Inc. referred to clubs that were already in existence as "unsanctioned, unauthorized, and unofficial." In an effort to win over some of these rogue players Tiffany wrote that there would be "expert points" given to designate various levels of Scrabble accomplishment, but "only members of Scrabble Players Clubs will be recognized and able to award Expert Points." It would be the scGP way or the highway. And it has pretty much been that way ever since. Stu Goldman, who started Club No. 5 on Long Island in 1974, recalls that s&R "wanted me to report any non-sanctioned clubs I heard about."

This situation existed, because unlike chess or checkers, Scrabble is trademarked. It was the property of s&R, which intended to protect it, because it claimed that the willy-nilly use of the mark could result in it becoming generic, and the company ultimately losing control of the game. The application to establish a club made that clear. The cost was twenty-five dollars, which included an annual licensing fee of ten dollars. Selchow & Righter was not giving the trademark away; it was licensing users.

It would appear that the architect of this scheme, probably Lee Tiffany, envisioned each club as a small business. The person who started the club was licensed and referred to as its owner. She was supposed to kick back to SCGP fifty cents per person for those attending each club session (twenty-five cents for closed clubs run by religious, fraternal, collegiate, or senior citizen organizations). It was left to the owner to decide what to charge club members per session, but SCGP suggested somewhere between fifty cents and three dollars. "About the price of a movie seems reasonable," suggested the *Scrabble Players Newspaper.* Presumably, the owner would pocket some percentage of that. Stu Goldman says he did and that the money came in handy during the rapid inflation in the late 1970s.

Senkiewicz says that some 200,000 players were expected to join clubs. If each of them played only twice a month, the clubs would remit $200,000 monthly to S&R. A cash cow. That rings true to Jim Houle. Early in the game, he says, S&R thought it could have a club on every corner. "They thought too, that they could make money by licensing clubs," he says. To him it sounds like a Tiffany scheme that would end up with the players generating the money to finance SCGP, with a good bit left over.

In fact, Senkiewicz says that 200,000 players was a conservative projection. "Selchow & Righter had sold some thirty million sets," he says, "and was selling a million or so a year." It was estimated that forty to fifty million people played at home. "If you just made one out of every 100 parlor players into serious players," says Senkiewicz, "then you could easily talk in terms of 200,000 club players." Dan Pratt, who played in Baltimore, says he was also optimistic. Chess had 29,000 rated players and Pratt expected Scrabble to overtake them. "Upon witnessing the enthusiasm at the early tournaments," says Pratt, "I thought we would be ahead of the chess world in just a few years and it was only a question of whether we would overtake bridge."

Nothing went as planned. The projections were greatly exaggerated. The players who did turn out weren't thrilled. Goldman says the kickback arrangement didn't go over well, either. "I paid the ten dollar licensing fee," says Goldman, "and the fifty cents per member fee, but only for the first session." Shortly thereafter, due to complaints, they were both dropped.

Something else that didn't get off the ground was a school Scrabble program. At the same time that SCGP announced that it would license regular clubs, it also made known that a Scrabble Players School Club manual was available. There were no weekly player kickbacks and teachers could purchase equipment at a discount. Once the clubs were established, according to the newsletter, "SCGP will begin interscholastic and regional competitions." This scheme resurfaced in the 1990s.

This was a turning point for the organized game. If players had packed the clubs and S&R had lined its coffers, the company might have put more money and effort into club and tournament Scrabble. But that didn't happen, so rather than a dynamic players' organization that was hellbent on expanding the game, SCGP became a low budget, poorly staffed, unimaginative operation, largely concerned with publicity and trademark protection. The result was a tension between the top players, who wanted the game to grow, and S&R, which couldn't see how to make money from the game, except by selling Scrabble sets, and so couldn't justify sinking cash into SCGP.

The regular clubs started slowly. There were nine in place by 1975, including one at the Kentucky State Penitentiary. This jumped to 100 by 1979. Gary Brown, who started the Brooklyn club, after playing at the Chess House and Chess City in Manhattan, says that advertising a club presented a damned-if-you-do-and-damned-if-you-don't dilemma. The clubs needed to do something to recruit members because S&R wasn't pulling its weight. Yet, if you tried to advertise, says Brown, "you might get slapped with a cease-and-desist letter from S&R that said, 'Don't misuse our name.'" All and all, he didn't think the company was very helpful.

If there were going to be clubs and tournaments, they needed rules. There were box top rules from the beginning, but they weren't up to the job of governing organized play, where matches had to move along quickly and there was no time to debate finer procedural points.

The first attempt at a rulebook was in *The Scrabble Players Handbook,* which came out in 1974. It was in chapter fourteen, called "Scrabble Players Tournament Rules." The rules addressed starting the game, time keeping, the dictionary, challenging words, how to position tiles, and scoring—essentially what is covered today, but it was done in about 1500 words, compared to today's roughly 5000.

There were some differences with contemporary rules. Today each player receives twenty-five minutes to play her game. This time can be used in large or small chunks. In contrast, the games in 1973 were governed by a master clock that allowed sixty minutes for both parties to finish. Individual moves, on the other hand, could take no more than three minutes as determined by a sand timer. Going over three minutes resulted in the loss of a turn.

Funk & Wagnalls College Dictionary, 1973 edition, was the official word source, with all the ambiguities inherent in a standard dictionary. How were disputes resolved? "The Tournament Director will be the final arbiter in all instances and will rule according to good English usage," said the rules. No one would be comfortable with that today, but there was no alternative prior to the development of an official word source specific to Scrabble.

The handbook instituted what is called "the double challenge rule." Under it, a player who challenges a word loses her turn if it is good, while if the word is incorrect, her opponent loses his turn. Scrabble was already played this way in the New York chess clubs, but this was not a box top rule. Today it is an integral part of the North American game, which makes the skillful playing of phony words an added arrow in the quiver of the expert player.

The handbook also dealt with bathroom breaks. No one ever wants to leave the tournament room during competition. The lines that form at the washrooms between games are ample evidence of that. Still, sometimes players have to answer the call. The penalty for doing so was much more severe in the 1970s than it is now. Today a player's clock is allowed to run while he is gone. All that is lost is the time away from the board. Not so in the handbook. A player could lose turns too (one every three minutes) and his opponent could play one or several times in his absence. "If a player must absent himself during the game, he will lose as many turns as it takes him to return.

A monitor will turn the absent player's timer and the opponent will continue to play." Ties were also handled differently. Instead of each player receiving half a game in the tournament standings as is done today, the person who had played the highest scoring word automatically won.

It would appear these rules did not get an overhaul until 1989. Whether they were all followed in practice is hard to say. Certainly tournament directors had more discretion than they do today. Some prohibited tile tracking, others penalized players fifty points for playing a phony blank (an upside-down tile), according to Joe Leonard, the Philadelphia word maven. No doubt there were also "local rules," and when official rules were seen as impediments to the game they were discarded.

In the interim, Alan Frank, the Boston area programmer who took over the job of calculating player ratings in 1984, came out with an extensive rulebook in 1985. As late as 1991 it was in its fifth printing, even though it was neither sanctioned by S&R, nor, after 1989, by Hasbro.

In 1987, John Williams, the new head of SCGP, attempted to get more player involvement in the administration of the game, with the hope of quelling the player grumbling that had caused his predecessor Jim Houle so much grief. One of the things he did was form a Rules Committee. This brought a greater degree of formalization to the game and reduced the discretion of tournament directors. When rules disputes arose, players had a better idea of what to expect, at the same time as they were treated more fairly. It was actually a boon for tournament directors too, because they could point to the rulebook in a contested situation and say, "Take it up with the Rules Committee."

There were other things happening in the late 1970s and early 1980s. The *Official Scrabble Players Dictionary* was published in 1978, an embryonic rating system appeared in 1980, thanks to Dan Pratt, and then was institutionalized in 1984 by Alan Frank. The number of tournaments gradually rose also, so that by 1986, when John Williams took over SCGP, there were seventy-five each year in the U.S.

3

Getting the Business

The Players Want a Voice

Credit must be given to S&R for getting serious Scrabble off the ground in 1973, but what has happened since then is largely due to the unflagging efforts of the players, with only a smidgeon of help from the owners. Arriving at this stage of the game's development had its ups and downs. Take the leadership of the company-owned players' organization, for example.

Lee Tiffany, the first head of Scrabble Crossword Game Players, left the group in 1976. This was after he agreed to an $11,000 settlement with Mark Landsberg, a California player, who had submitted a how-to Scrabble manuscript to S&R. The manuscript never saw the light of day, but S&R published a similar book entitled the *Scrabble Players Handbook* shortly thereafter, which gave rise to Landsberg's suit. The incident suggested that the players and the owner were both allies and adversaries in the struggle to establish the game.

Tiffany was followed by James Tobias, who had a brief stint at the helm before he too was sacked. In 1976 Jim Houle was given his marching orders by Ellsworth Tobias himself. Houle was told, "I want you to fix up SCGP," which was a reference to the Tiffany and Tobias problems. Houle was another unusual candidate for the job. With a master's degree in chemical engineering, he had kicked around the private sector for twenty-four years prior to landing in S&R's factory. He had worked for the 3M Company, American Viscose, and Mobil Chemical, among others.

Besides protecting the trademark, Houle saw his job as promoting the game. When he made a corporate accounting to the board of directors, one of the major things he pointed to, just as John Williams of the National Scrabble Association does today, is the number of Scrabble-related articles published in newspapers and magazines—free publicity. When he worked to enlarge the SCGP membership, what he had as his goal was publicity, not building the organized game. His goal was 10,000 players, although his high point was 3900. "I figured if I had 10,000 that would be enough to get a consistent reporting of tournaments throughout the country. That's an awful lot of press," says Houle.

Houle's tenure at SCGP inspired strong opinions among the letterati and still does. In fairness, he did inaugurate the North American Invitational in 1978, a tournament that would eventually become the Nationals, the high point of competitive Scrabble today. He was also around when the rating system was started, when the number of clubs was growing rapidly, and when the *Official Scrabble Players Dictionary* debuted. Yet true or not, there was the

Day 1 of the 1978 North American Invitational in New York. From front to back on the left side of the table are Roz Grossman, Ed Hepner, Mike Senkiewicz. John Ozag is shaking hands with Roz, behind him is Tim Maneth, about to play Hepner. Then Frank Khuenrich is waiting for his opponent, and Dan Pratt is playing Senkiewicz.

perception among many of the players that Houle was not the man for the job.

Houle recalls that he had problems keeping up the membership. Once it reached 3900 it began to tail off. "We had the same hardcore of 2000 or so," he says, "while the others would come and go." In retrospect he thinks part of the problem was the *Scrabble Players Newspaper* (SPN), which he feels was over the heads of most newcomers to the game. "People would join," says Houle, "and then wonder why they were spending five dollars for a newsletter that was beyond them." This is quite the opposite of the thinking of many of the better players, who considered the publication too elementary. It highlights the differing goals of Houle and the letterati. The former was only interested in publicity, while the latter wanted to grow the game.

Today, a sampling of opinion about Houle runs the gamut. Charles Goldstein, who was a strong player on the national scene from 1978–85, says, "Houle was a corporate person with no background in games. He strung people along and was unreliable." As if that weren't enough, Goldstein is still chafed over the newsletter. "The SPN was terrible under Houle," says Goldstein. "This was a publication for word people that sometimes had a hundred typos." In those days Goldstein was so upset with the situation at SCGP that he sometimes wore a hat to tournaments which flaunted the phrase "DUMP THE ASSHOULE."

Ron Tiekert, a New York player at the time, is less critical. He thinks Houle was never suited to the job, but says, "I didn't read malice or reckless disregard into his actions. I found him pleasant on a personal level." Joe Leonard of Philadelphia, who created scores of word lists for Houle to publish in the SPN, has similar memories. Houle was never a strong leader, says Leonard, and in fact, was a people pleaser. "He would say different things to different people, things he thought they wanted to hear."

Perhaps Houle's biggest problem was his inability to get the newsletter out on time, which in the pre-Internet days was the only source of Scrabble information for the membership. Joe Leonard, who was a regular contributor to the SPN and frequently corresponded with Houle, remembers it this way. S&R required SCGP to operate on a limited budget. Houle, for example, had to mail the SPN bulk rate, which could mean some of them bounced around the postal system for up to six weeks. On top of that, says Leonard, "Houle was not in good health." He apparently had some irreversible disorder, says Leonard, and winter hit him hard. This came to the fore in February 1985, when Houle failed to put out an important issue of the SPN that was supposed to contain North American Championship qualifying information. He apologized by saying, "the weather on Long Island was cold and icy . . . a perfect combination for the virus. From December to early February most of the staff was out sick, either with laryngitis or relapses or both."

Al Weissman, who with his wife Donna put out their own Scrabble newsletter, *Letters for Expert Game Players*, got drawn into this. His experience probably reflects the frustration that many players of the time experienced. It was assumed that there would be qualifying tournaments prior to the 1985 Nationals. They had been announced, but the "where" and "when" were unclear. Weissman had missed out on the 1983 event because he had gotten the qualifying information too late to rearrange his work schedule. So in 1985 he wrote Houle pleading for help. His response trickled in five weeks later, just two weeks prior to the Northeast qualifying event, and he was livid over what he perceived as bungling at SCGP. He wrote in his newsletter, "When will Scrabble, renamed generically, ever belong to the players," who he felt would solve many of these problems.

The 1985 SPN debacle proved to be the last straw for Richard Selchow, who ran the company. The newsletter was supposed to showcase the 1985 North American Scrabble Open (NASO), the crown jewel in S&R's PR efforts. In fact, the newsletter was probably the only reason most players remained members of SCGP.

Al Weissman at the Game Room, playing in a preliminary
round, day 1 of a tournament held in December 1979.

So in 1985 a part-time PR/marketing guy and sometimes novel writer named John Williams, who had been
doing projects for S&R since the 1983 Nationals, convinced S&R that the newsletter was pretty bad. Dick

Selchow asked Williams to take it over. Williams thought he could get it out on time, which hadn't happened for a while. Content was another matter. "I had a lot to learn about Scrabble," says Williams, who would make his share of gaffes over the next few years.

On August 1, 1985, the day after the North American Scrabble Open, a Scrabble Symposium was held at the Boston Sheraton Hotel with John Williams chairing and Richard Selchow, along with John Nason, the vice president for marketing at s&r, in attendance. For the first time in the history of the game they sought advice from players and club directors.

The minutes of that meeting show that the players gave s&r management an earful about Houle, the newsletter, the mismanaged Nationals, the lack of Scrabble books, and the paucity of support for tournament Scrabble. "The seeds of having the players involved with the association were planted," says Mike Baron, of Albuquerque, New Mexico, who was in attendance. Houle was not there, which was a sign that his days at scgp were numbered.

s&r had created the problem. It ran the players' organization on the cheap, even to the point of wanting it to pay its own way. The idea that the letterati might take the game and the organization seriously was probably never anticipated. It would appear that s&r wanted PR from the clubs and tournaments and a loose framework for controlling the game which would, if need be, provide evidence in a court of law that it was policing its trademark. Only the players wanted to grow the game.

Not long after the symposium Houle was out and Williams was in. Houle became the publisher emeritus of the SPN and Williams the publisher. Houle wrote a few editorials, Williams put together a laudatory article about him in the January 1986 issue and then Houle dropped further and further into the background. In the same issue, the SPN was called "newly redesigned and revamped" by Richard Selchow who wrote a short editorial. He blamed the 1985 North American Scrabble Open preparations for the previous year's newsletter delays and promised SPN would be "bigger, livelier, better, and more timely—than ever." A new era had begun but the changes were minor compared to what was about to shake the small world of organized Scrabble.

In 1986, Coleco Industries, riding high with the Cabbage Patch Doll, bought the assets of S&R. The Selchow family wanted out of the business, according to Williams. Selchow & Righter was flush due to the revenues from Trivial Pursuit, and the sale allowed most senior executives to cash out and retire. But this plunged competitive Scrabble into limbo. A few months after taking over, says Williams, the Coleco VP for marketing announced they were disbanding SCGP, firing everyone, and moving to Connecticut. Then Williams was told that he could run an independent, partially subsidized group if he wanted to. Why Williams? According to him, departing S&R executives, particularly Dick Selchow and the VP for marketing, John Nason, recommended him, and he got on well with the Coleco execs during the transition.

After laying out plans for a 1987 Nationals, Coleco postponed the event to 1988. It was laboring to crack the home computer market with its Adam machine, at the same time as it hemorrhaged money, says Williams. By June 1987, the situation had deteriorated to the point that Williams found it necessary to write a piece in SPN on the future of the organized game.

The good news was that the dust had settled after the Coleco takeover and the SCGP organization would continue. The bad news was that his budget had been cut, the North American Scrabble Open cancelled, and the *SPN* cut back to a quarterly. Trying to put the best face on the situation he said, "That's reality, it's over, and now it's time to look ahead."

According to the *SPN*, Williams wanted to pay regional directors to oversee tournaments. On top of that, Coleco was looking for a major corporate co-sponsor for the Nationals, wanted to give more autonomy to the clubs, and also encourage the writing of Scrabble how-to books, something that S&R had all but prevented. It also intended to look into revising the *Official Scrabble Players Dictionary*, which was long overdue. These were issues the letterati wanted addressed. Williams encouraged the membership to write him with their questions.

Things got worse before they got better. An *SPN* came out in September of 1987 and then the publication went silent until the March 1988 issue. After eighteen months of uncertainty, Williams reported a further reorganization. Williams and Company had signed an agreement with Coleco. He would handle SCGP, publish the newsletter, and put on the Nationals, which would take place in Reno in 1988. *Scrabble Players Newspaper* would resume as a quarterly publication, the dictionary would be updated, they would revise the rules, launch a school Scrabble program, and kick off a membership drive. In a further effort to make points with the players, he announced that in February 1988, Joe Edley, the winner of the 1980 North American Invitational, was hired as VP for Clubs and

Tournaments. This brought actual knowledge of the game to SCGP, something it had lacked throughout most of its fifteen-year existence.

Williams says now that he had a number of goals at the time, all intended to bump up his credibility in the eyes of the members. These included increasing player involvement by establishing an Advisory Board, which was followed by a Rules Committee and later a Dictionary Committee. He also wanted to get the SPN out on time, improve the rating system and, under Joe Edley's tutelage, become a better player himself.

Yet it wasn't long before Coleco was in reorganization—chapter 11 bankruptcy. According to a letter from Edley in November of 1988, they were still holding on, but Williams had personally lost money and Edley himself was getting paid much less than his agreed-upon salary. Before things settled down Williams would be out thousands of dollars. Nevertheless, they were committed to making the organization work, wrote Edley, and were awaiting the outcome of Coleco's efforts to get on its feet.

When Coleco's reorganization fell short in 1989, its assets were acquired by Milton Bradley, a subsidiary of Hasbro, and Williams got a new boss. "We were out of business for six months after Coleco failed," says Williams. During that time he tried not to let anyone know how bad things were "for fear of panic and defection." Williams covered SCGP salaries and the costs of the SPN out of his own pocket. "Coleco stuck me personally for about $13,000, which I never got back," he says. Rather than getting out, though, Williams hung on. "I'd become genuinely interested in the Scrabble world," he says. "I was hoping to get back some of the money I'd lost too."

1992 Nationals in Atlanta. From left to right, Mark Nyman, Stan Rubinsky, Joe Edley, Peter Morris. Edley doing a "how the game was won" bit just after his victory against Wapnick was secured. Morris and Nyman were playing in the tournament; Rubinsky was the director.

Contrary to the stated goal, *SPN* was only published sporadically in those days: two issues in 1988, three in 1989, and finally four in 1990. At the same time, Edley, who has never had the PR instincts of Williams, was seen by many players as spending too much of his time playing in tournaments. He also aggravated SCGP members and tournament directors with what some have called a brusque personal style. He seemed to have no people skills. This reached a head in 1990 when a petition was circulated that asked for Edley's removal. Some time later his job description changed, which also altered his duties. This secured his position and made life easier for all concerned.

The ups and downs further weakened the membership to around 2200. So when Milton Bradley took over, George Ditomassi, the president, felt it was necessary to send out a letter in December 1989 to the 15,000 or so people who had been SCGP members over the years. He assured them "that we plan to strengthen our ties with all your interests and events and continue their sponsorship." He said he would take a personal interest in SCGP. "Please bear with us," he wrote, "as we strive to bring back the best."

At the same time, says Williams, he had to convince Ditomassi to put Williams and Company under contract to run SCGP. Since then he has had to make his case to Milton Bradley on a yearly basis to obtain funding. "Basically we do it every year by getting publicity." For example, when he took over in 1986 there were seventy-five tournaments. By 1999 that number had climbed to 175, thanks to the players. Some of these events generate news stories, some 300 in 1999. Every time they do, Hasbro receives free ink and SCGP, and later the National Scrabble Association (NSA), its successor, is seen as pulling its share of the PR load.

Sometime around 1990 (Williams isn't sure) SCGP became the National Scrabble Association. "The name is simpler and more marketable than SCGP," says Williams. He upped the membership too. By 1991 the turmoil of the late 1980s had taken its toll, with the roster dropping from a high of 3900 to a low of 2200. Shortly thereafter, Williams announced that to play in a sanctioned tournament a person had to be a member of the NSA. Practically overnight the membership jumped to 4000. This has since risen to around 10,000, according to Williams, although no one knows for sure and many players who follow the scene feel those figures are inflated.

Still, the NSA staff is growing and taking on more tasks. The Scrabble in the Schools Program was resurrected in 1991 and given more emphasis recently. "It represents the future of the game," says Williams. The amount of money Hasbro put into Scrabble also increased in the 1990s. They feel the PR from the clubs and tournaments sells games, says Williams. The staff at the National Scrabble Association has jumped to three full-time and four part-timers. Jane Williams, John's wife, has become Director of Operations. The NSA has a website. Scrabble tournaments have been on ESPN a few times.

Scrabble and the NSA are joined at the hip, but the organized game doesn't need to grow any more than it has to accomplish the goals set out for it by S&R back in 1973—namely to sell games and protect the trademark. It might even be argued that if organized Scrabble grows too much, the job of protecting the trademark will become increasingly more difficult with more power devolving to the players, demands for outside sponsorship, and all the labor/management disagreements that have become com monplace in mainline sports.

4

The Last Word

Scrabble Gets a Dictionary

The *Official Club and Tournament Word List* (OWL) is the bible for organized Scrabble. Some players criticize it because the words are either too weird or too common. Others lament that it's not a real dictionary with definitions. Still others want to add the British word list to it, 30,000 words or so. But the OWL is the only word and the last word in North America. Anyone who wants to play competitively accepts it. A word is in the book or it isn't. Most of the letterati get on with their Scrabble lives and leave the kvetching to others. They recognize that there has to be a standard. Anyone who has tried to play without one quickly realizes that.

The New York chess club players understood this and adopted *Funk & Wagnalls College Dictionary* in the 1960s. Ann Sanfedele remembers it this way. She lived with Richie Gilston, who at one point was an editor at

Funk & Wagnalls. Gilston was also one of the first serious players of the game. He never competed in tournaments but did play for money.

Sometime in the 1960s, says Sanfedele, they acknowledged the need for a single word source. Gilston was in favor of an unabridged dictionary, she says, because he was a well-educated, literary kind of guy with a large vocabulary. This mattered because few players studied word lists. An unabridged dictionary would have given Gilston a leg up. The other players, however, were gamers, not intellectuals, and nixed the unabridged idea, says Sanfedele. "So from Gilston's point of view they settled on *Funk & Wagnalls* as being the best of a bad lot," she says.

It had some nice qualities, as far as the players were concerned, says Dan Pratt, of Maryland, who has followed the dictionary question for three decades. It had oodles of words with UN-, RE-, MIS-, OUT-, and OVER- prefixes, as well as many obviously foreign words. When S&R set up Scrabble Crossword Game Players, Inc. to license clubs and sanction tournaments in 1973, it followed precedent and declared *Funk & Wagnalls* its official dictionary, probably because it was the easiest thing to do.

Funk & Wagnalls had its problems. It was a real dictionary. To find some words a person had to know where to look. Take ZOA, says Carol Felstein Vignet, who used *Funk & Wagnalls* in the mid 1970s when she was a word judge at the Brooklyn tournaments. "If you didn't know that ZOA was the plural of ZOON," says Vignet, "you wouldn't find it," because it was under ZOON.

Joe Leonard, of Philadelphia, says that wasn't all. *Funk & Wagnalls* didn't put foreign words in italics, he says, so words like BITTE, JA, and OUI were considered good

Scrabble words. It also had many words that lacked parts of speech, says Leonard, trademarked terms that were not capitalized, and one-syllable adjectives, which made words like MAINEST (MAIN, MAINER, MAINEST) good. Vignet says there was a whole set of conventions that had been developed in the chess clubs that made it generally clear which words took -S or -ER and such, but that sometimes she had to rely on good English usage in her decisions.

Ann Sanfedele remembers that some word judges didn't know the conventions, nor were they sufficiently familiar with *Funk & Wagnalls* to adjudicate tournaments with any consistency. She says that many players wanted a straightforward easy-to-use dictionary.

Mike Senkiewicz proposed such a volume to S&R around 1975. The idea was to compile it from four or five standard college dictionaries and call it the *Official Scrabble Players Dictionary*. The dictionary would increase the total number of playable words, clarify how words were pluralized and used in comparisons, and put all the words in alphabetical order. This would eliminate the idiosyncrasies of *Funk & Wagnalls*, so just about anyone could use it.

But according to Shazzi Felstein, who lived with Senkiewicz at the time, there was one problem. Senkiewicz felt S&R wasn't offering him enough money to do the job. Felstein would have assisted in the compilation and says, "I was dying to do it." She thought that it would improve her game dramatically. "I said, 'Mike, please take this money, no one will ever beat me again'," says Felstein, who now lives in Florida. But he didn't, which he has always suspected was what S&R wanted, so that the company could compile it for less. Which it did.

When touting the dictionary in the April 1978 *SPN*, Jim Houle wrote, "What an array of etymologists, linguists, lexicographers, editors and proof readers they [G. and C. Merriam] put to work for you." In fact, the people who compiled the dictionary were young Scrabble players employed by Werewick, Welsh and Miller, a PR firm hired by S&R to promote events and tournaments. According to David Prinz, the primary editor of the dictionary and winner of the 1978 National Invitational Championship, S&R viewed compilation of the dictionary as part of its PR mission—a way to sell more Scrabble sets.

Jonathan Hatch, who won the first Brooklyn tournament in 1973, and who promoted Scrabble for S&R, was one of the player/editors too. According to Hatch, he and his girlfriend Kathy Flaherty initially met with Lee Tiffany and his assistant Drue Conklin to set up guidelines for the project. "Tiffany and Conklin didn't know much about the game," says Hatch, "but they said they wanted to make this an inclusive dictionary to give Scrabble players more opportunities and either we or they decided on the five dictionaries that were eventually scoured for words." Hatch never met anyone from G. and C. Merriam.

Hatch remembers it as "a great gig." He and Flaherty were twenty-seven-year-old singers who toured college campuses. "It allowed us to pursue our own thing and yet we had this great job," says Hatch. For two years they worked on the dictionary in hotel rooms from coast to coast. "They hired us," says Hatch, "because they didn't want to pay royalties." The pair rummaged through dictionaries for usable words, defined as those that were eight letters or less, not obviously foreign, not capitalized and so on. If a word appeared in any of the five source dictionaries it got included in the master list. They wrote up definitions, jotted everything onto legal pads, and submitted them to Drue Conklin at SCGP.

David Prinz edited the words. He had played in the first Brooklyn tournament, occasionally at the Game Room, and had become friends with Drue Conklin at SCGP because he wrote a column for SPN. It was a dream gig for Prinz too. He was twenty-one when it started, just out of college, and had no desire to get a nine-to-five job. "It was two and a half years of fun," says Prinz. He worked at home but took it very seriously. "It was going to be the official word source," he says, "and I thought it was important that it tied together on all levels."

He began by editing the lists Hatch and Flaherty had compiled using *Funk & Wagnalls Standard College Dictionary*, 1973; G. and C. Merriam's eighth *Webster's Collegiate*, 1973; the *Random House College Dictionary*, 1968; *Webster's New World Dictionary*, second college edition, 1970; and the *American Heritage Dictionary of the English Language*, 1969. Prinz used the unabridged *Webster's Third New International Dictionary*, 1966, to check for inflections that were not included in the other sources.

Prinz says that he paraphrased dictionary definitions to avoid legal problems: the company that assiduously protected its trademark didn't want to get caught poaching. "The definitions had to be concise," says Prinz. Hatch recalls that he and Flaherty put in some definitions that were inside jokes that only they understood.

Prinz was the only one to visit G. and C. Merriam. He would submit questions when none of the five dictionaries contained the answers for difficult usages. A Merriam editor, James Lowe, would consult citation files from books, magazines, and newspapers to see how the word had been used. "Sometimes it was just an educated guess," says Prinz, "because they didn't have any citations." But generally he feels that Merriam was a big help.

Prinz worked on one letter at a time. Then his girl-friend typed up the words as they would eventually appear in the OSPD. They got paid a letter at a time, from A to Z. He doesn't think he was edited and regrets that. "Merriam worked with me on some plurals and declensions, but otherwise it was printed intact," he says. James Lowe, senior editor at what is now Merriam-Webster, remembers it that way too. He not only worked on OSPD1 but also later editions. "We accepted the manuscript as it was," says Lowe. "We did try to eliminate foreign words and abbreviations and we checked to see if the words were in the original dictionaries."

There were mixed reactions to the dictionary. Carol Felstein Vignet remembers that some players didn't like it because it wasn't a real dictionary—the definitions were too short. Others objected because it leveled the playing field. They would have to start studying all over again. Jim Pate, of Birmingham, Alabama, recalls that former New York City champ Frank Kuehnrich quit playing because of it. But Pate says, "I really liked it because it had a lot of new words." Stu Goldman, of New York at the time, also remembers the switch fondly. He says the additional words were welcomed by most. Clubs and tournaments officially adopted the OSPD October 1, 1978, he says. "In a sense we learned the words together."

No one at S&R ever talked to Prinz, Hatch, or Flaherty about the final product. Nor did the team get any feedback from G. and C. Merriam. They didn't get any credit for the dictionary, either, other than a one-paragraph blurb in the newsletter. This, even though Lee Tiffany had promised them that their names would be prominently displayed in the OSPD. Jim Houle, who took over SCGP about a year after Tiffany's departure, says that he did put the names of Prinz, Hatch, Flaherty, and Bernie Teitelbaum of Yonkers, who did a little editing, on a draft of the dictionary. "The lawyers said, no, you can't do that," says Houle.

Hatch feels they should have sued, but Prinz is glad he didn't. He feels his entire life flowed from the project. In 1978 S&R offered him another gig, this time as an expert witness in the Landsberg case, in which Landsberg, a player, sued the company for stealing his book idea. Again Prinz made good money working at home and $300 a day at the trial, even though he never testified. Because of his expert witness status, he was invited to the 1978 North American Invitational—and won. He got his first real job because a recruiter was gaga over his Scrabble prowess. One of his coworkers on the new job convinced him to go into business and the rest is history. He ended up owning two of the largest music stores in the country.

Hatch and Flaherty did okay too. In 1980 they used their Scrabble money to buy a summer house that they still own and refer to as their "Scrabble house." It also worked out well for SCGP, according to Houle. The money from the royalties on the OSPD went to finance the organization. In a sense, SCGP had become self-supporting, just as Lee Tiffany had hoped at its inception.

As the years passed, people voiced dissatisfaction with the *Official Scrabble Players Dictionary*. Why wasn't this or that old or new word included? There were new editions of the source dictionaries; wasn't it time to cull those dictionaries for new words? It fell to Joe Leonard, a resident of Philadelphia and tenacious word maven, to accomplish that task. Like Prinz, Hatch, and Flaherty before him, though, he never received any credit. And if that wasn't bad enough, he wasn't paid.

With Leonard it started small, but his obsession with words grew, until in 1988 Mike Baron, compiler of *The Wordbook*, referred to him as "The Listmaster General." Leonard has contributed as much to the organized game of Scrabble as anyone, yet today only the old-timers know who he is. He keeps a low profile, lives alone, spends modestly, and follows the Scrabble world through extensive correspondence, since he doesn't have a phone, much less e-mail. Over the past several years, for example, we've exchanged over thirty letters. He still types on a manual machine, sometimes in considerable pain, if he has been out on a cold Philadelphia day.

His interest in words extends beyond Scrabble. Without computer assistance, he compiled lists of words that contain A, E, I, O, and U palindromes (words that read the same both forward and backward). He also has developed lists ending in -OLOGY, -OGRAPHY, -OMANCY and much more. He has an interest in pseudonyms, rhyming words, American Indian words, and place names too. When he learned that I had lived in Hawaii, references to Hawaiian words and place names began to crop up in his letters. It was this passion for words that he brought to the Scrabble world.

He first played Scrabble in 1950 with relatives. During the 1960s and '70s he wrote technical specifications, largely for dental equipment and chemical processes, for the federal government, and also played a friendly game of Scrabble from time to time. Leonard was drawn to the OSPD when it came out in 1978, even though he was neither a club- nor tournament-goer. He was a good speller, though, and with his eye for detail found some typos and out-of-order entries, that he sent along to Jim Houle at SCGP. "I wanted the dictionary to be as nearly perfect as possible," he says, a trait that would characterize his efforts for the next twenty-five years.

Leonard discovered that Scrabble players liked word lists and he liked making them. It wasn't long before his labors appeared in the *Scrabble Players Newspaper*. At first he worked with six- and seven-letter words and in 1979 began the prodigious task of putting the 21,733 seven-letter words contained in the *Official Scrabble Players Dictionary* in alpha order. "I would type the word, alphabetize it (ZYZZYVA [a tropical weevil] became AVYYZZZ), and put it in one of 26 baggies," says Leonard.

His revisions of the OSPD began independently, like all his work, as early as 1979. He first noticed that some eligible words had been skipped. He already owned the *American Heritage Dictionary* and *Webster's New Collegiate*, eighth edition. He bought *Webster's New World Dictionary* and the *Random House College Dictionary*. Someone gave him a *Funk & Wagnalls* (from which he extracted words that, in the end, were not used).

By mid 1982 he had scoured all the dictionaries and had about 2000 new words. "S&R was not the least bit interested," says Leonard, "since it would cost them money to publish a revised dictionary." Possibly because of Leonard's work, Jim Houle did create a Dictionary Committee in 1983. Houle also says that he passed Leonard's revisions on to G. and C. Merriam, which included some of them in later printings of the OSPD when they could be squeezed onto existing pages in the original format, nicely sidestepping the added expense of a revised edition.

Also in 1983 Merriam published the ninth edition of *Webster's New Collegiate Dictionary*. Leonard went back to work. He typed up his new-found nuggets in April 1985. Time passed. Coleco bought out S&R, thus acquiring Scrabble, John Williams took over SCGP from Jim Houle in late 1985, and Joe Edley was hired in February 1988 as vice president in charge of clubs and tournaments. In March of 1988 Edley sent a note to Leonard in which he explained that he was interested in the list of new words. What happened next is a tragedy. Although Leonard devoted some 8000 hours to the revision of the OSPD, what could then have been a grand moment, completely disintegrated.

In April 1988, Leonard sent Edley his list of close to 5000 new words. Edley began retyping them but only reached the Cs before pooping out. He gave the task over to Karen Merrill of the Portland, Oregon, club, who had volunteered to help. In the meantime the third edition of *Webster's New World Dictionary* was published, making the Leonard/Merrill list obsolete. Leonard set to work on the *Webster's*, discovered some 700 new words, added them to his previous 5000, and typed up a forty-four page, two-column list from AARGH to ZYMOSANS. He sent them to Edley in May of 1989 and Edley responded, "What an effort! Scrabble players will be indebted to you and your work will not go uncredited." He added, "I know you cannot accept money, but if there is anything we can do for you, just name it, and if we can, we will." But they never did. (Leonard doesn't know where Edley got the idea that he couldn't accept money.)

He heard from Edley about something else, though. Could he put the words in a different format for Merriam-Webster? This would entail the addition of definitions and parts of speech, as well as dealing with new comparatives, superlatives, and nouns such as NUKE, which had changed to verbs, as well as cross-referencing. Then there was retyping, and this was all supposed to be done in two to three months, according to Leonard. Looking back on it, he says "I could never have done it without suffering complete mental burnout." He told Edley no, "and so there was increasing animosity between Edley and me," says Leonard.

In the meantime Coleco went under, Milton Bradley, an arm of Hasbro, bought Scrabble and decided to go ahead with the OSPD revision with Merriam-Webster. A few months later Edley threw Leonard a curve. In a laudatory story about Karen Merrill in the SPN for January of 1990, among other things Edley thanked her for "helping move forward the publishing date of the revised OSPD. . . ." There was no mention of Leonard and in retrospect Merrill says she found the whole article a little embarrassing. Whether it was Edley's intent to slight Leonard or just fill column inches, we'll never know. He hadn't said much, but for Leonard it was far too much. He was livid.

During the same period an irritated Leonard sent Merrill insulting correspondence, which she says disrupted her life for the better part of a year. He later apologized, but still got into hot water when Merrill forwarded the correspondence to Edley.

At the same time as all of this was going on, there were also obscene phone calls to Milton Bradley staff, which were attributed to Leonard, but which he denies. "I don't even have a phone," says Leonard. In 1991, the same year as the OSPD2 was published, the NSA revoked Leonard's membership. He was ostracised. There was one consolation, though; James Lowe, the OSPD editor at Merriam-Webster, sent Leonard a complimentary copy of the dictionary. None of Milton Bradley's representatives saw fit to bother.

Leonard never asked for any money, nor was any offered, although he says now that both Jim Houle and Joe Edley said he would be paid. There was ample precedent for this, since Leonard had been paid for numerous smaller lists that had appeared in SPN over the years. There was no contract, not even a hand shake, but that's Joe Leonard. No one has ever called him an astute businessman.

Leonard had no contract, kept to himself, was poor and going through a rough patch. It was doubtful that he would seek a legal remedy. Under the circumstances one can surmise that it made good business sense to sweep him under the rug and hope that he would stay there. Which he did, except when it came to his principal mission of revising the OSPD. His work continued.

A fair question would be why. Looking back, he says, "I didn't consider the 1990 event worthy of being called a big blowup, even though it does seem to have turned out that way." He thought that in a short time the NSA would reinstate him. After all, he had compiled their word lists and revised their dictionary on an ongoing basis for over ten years. He even expected that he would get credit for his work on the *OSPD* revision.

When the tenth edition of *Webster's* was published in April of 1993, he bought it. At the time he was recovering from skin cancer surgery, still enjoyed compiling lists, and found that "culling the Tenth" was a way to stay occupied and to do something for his many friends in Scrabble. In 1995, when the *OSPD3* (the expurgated *OSPD2*, plus a few additional words) was published, he saw that it did not contain his newfound words, some 165, from ADZUKI to YUPS (these two words are now acceptable). Leonard realized the NSA would not deal with him, so he slipped the words to Stu Goldman of San Francisco, who passed them on to Joe Edley, who published them in the December 1995 *Scrabble News*. They appeared without comment or attribution. That was fine with Leonard. "The list was not doing anyone any good just being a part of my files," he says.

After the Merrill incident, Leonard became a nonperson at the NSA. But in early 2000 he was reinstated. He now has a legitimate subscription to *SPN*, as opposed to the sub rosa one that kept him informed after his banishment. Could recognition be far behind? Well, yes. When asked if a laudatory article in *SPN* might be possible, John Williams replied that he doubted that the company's legal department, which reviews all *SPN* material before it is published, would agree to such a thing.

Some thirty years ago, according to Jim Houle, it was the lawyers at S&R who wouldn't allow the names of David Prinz, Jonathan Hatch, Kathy Flaherty, and Bernie Teitelbaum to appear on the original *OSPD*. Was it about the money? And is it still about the money? Might the original compilers in the 1970s, and Joe Leonard today, have some claim on a portion of the royalties from the OSPD if their work were formally acknowledged by the company? That's a question for the lawyers too.

Dirty Words and SOWPODS Too

Expurgation and the Brits

At the heart of Scrabble is the lexicon. Anyone who wants to tamper with it should keep that in mind. This was never more evident than in 1994 when Milton Bradley/Hasbro announced that it intended to expurgate the *Official Scrabble Players Dictionary* (OSPD2) of salacious, derogatory, and four-letter words. In the minds of the letterati this gave rise to images of political correctness, thought police, and Orwell's *1984*.

Actually, Scrabble players have never used all the words, whether in *Funk & Wagnalls* or the OSPD. The rules don't allow one-letter, hyphenated, italicized, capitalized, and most foreign words, or words with apostrophes. But there is something about offensive words that brings out the protectiveness in the letterati. They may not use them that often in conversation, or even over the board, but ban them? Never. David Prinz recalls, for example, that *Funk & Wagnalls* contained BLOWJOB, so he just followed the agreed-upon guidelines when he included it in the original OSPD in 1978 and it remains in the *Official Club and Tournament Word List* (OWL) to this day (the list used by club and tournament players).

Scrabble players are fond of saying that words are just game pieces. They are played devoid of meaning, except to the most thin-skinned. So over the board blacks are not bothered by DARKIES, whites by OFAY, Jews by JEWING, or Italians by DAGO. They are just words, a means of scoring points. Well, almost. There are occasions where a particular word makes a player feel uncomfortable. I know some words have made me a little squeamish. I've heard a nervous "sorry" before CUNT hit the board, and one time in post-game conversation a Japanese-American woman assured me she hadn't meant anything when she played OFAY. But this is the exception. The majority of the time, with the majority of players, the only consideration is what is the strategically best word to play.

Not so in the real world, where use of these terms can offend and worse. Or for that matter, when the Scrabble world and the real world intersect. In 1990, for example, after winning the National Scrabble Championship, the late Bob Felt appeared on *Good Morning America*. He showed the reconstructed board for his last round and defined a number of the words he had played. What the audience didn't know was that Felt had changed the word DARKIES TO DARKENS. What was fine in the world of Scrabble was not so fine on national TV. Felt said it was his idea and that he would do it again. "I didn't think that defining that word on national television was in anybody's interest," he said. So it should come as no surprise that

Bob Felt (L) and Bob Lipton (R) at table 3 at the Masters
Tournament in 1991 in Cincinnati.

people outside of the competitive game might want to go
even further. Which gets us to the great expurgation.

There are two explanations for it. One is documented,
one a rumor. Let's start with the rumor. As the story
goes, someone high up in the Hasbro organization, who
was not a player, was made aware in 1994 that the OSPD2
contained the word KIKE. This person became irate and
ordered that KIKE and other derogatory terms be
removed. There's no verification of this episode, but it
continues to kick around the Scrabble world. It contains
an element of plausibility, since the company is owned by
the Hassenfeld family, which has been active in various
Jewish causes for three decades. What's more, John
Williams, head of the National Scrabble Association, has

confirmed such a complaint, but contends that it had nothing to do with the expurgation.

The other story, backed by John Williams, involves Judith Grad, a resident of McLean, Virginia. Supposedly, while she was visiting friends in Baltimore who were holocaust survivors, the subject of Scrabble came up and her friends brought out their OSPD2. As Grad browsed the volume she came across the word JEW used as a verb. She found it offensive and decided to do something about it.

According to an article in the Springfield, Virginia, *Connection* for June 2, 1994, she wrote letters to Milton Bradley and Merriam-Webster, but got no satisfaction. E. David Wilson, the president of MB, replied, "As a dictionary it is a reflection of words currently used in our language. It is important to note that MB does not condone the use of these words, nor do we advocate the use of offensive terms." This riled Grad even more. She contacted the NAACP, the Anti-Defamation League, the Zionists Organization of America, and local media figures. When she again failed to get satisfaction, she undertook a countrywide letter writing campaign through the National Council of Jewish Women.

Whether or not Grad made an impact isn't clear. She thinks she did and she certainly stirred the pot. The Anti-Defamation League got involved, but there doesn't seem to be a paper trail to Grad's door. Myrna Scheinbaum of the ADL's New York City office doesn't recall her name, but does remember ADL's role. How it came to their attention, Scheinbaum isn't sure. She is certain, though, that on March 22, 1994, Jeffrey Sinensky, ADL's director of civil rights, fired off a letter to Alan Hassenfeld, Chairman and CEO of Hasbro, the parent company of

Milton Bradley. "The use of ethnic slurs in Scrabble," wrote Sinensky, "is literally playing games with hate." In particular he objected to their use "in a book that serves as a parlor game guide that is often used by children." Sinensky asked that the derogatory terms be "retired to the recreational dustbin."

Within three weeks, Donald Robbins, Senior VP and General Counsel for Hasbro, wrote to Sinensky. He said that MB had been concerned about some of the words in the OSPD but also had to consider the players and their first amendment rights. Still, the ADL letter had "stimulated management to reexamine the issues," wrote Robbins. It now concurred with the ADL's position and the objectionable words would be removed in the September printing.

This was a business decision. The ADL could bring the company a great deal of negative publicity. Already there were unflattering articles in the Jewish press. All Hasbro needed was a spate of publicity that indicted the company for bigotry. No doubt the trademark holder wanted to get the whole mess behind it and get on with selling games.

The players first learned about all of this in the *Scrabble News* (formerly the *Scrabble Players Newspaper*). Neither opinions nor suggestions were solicited. The expurgation of racial slurs, obscenities, vulgarities, swear words, and unflattering references would go forward, according to the article, probably penned by John Williams. That was it. Fifty to one hundred words had to go because the company had received complaints. And if that weren't sufficient justification, there was also the proposed Scrabble in the Schools program to think about. To sell more games, the company planned to get children playing during school time. The article said that in preparation for this, parents, teachers, and educational consultants (probably lawyers too) had recommended a similar expurgation.

John Williams, NSA executive director, tried to explain the decision in an editorial. He opposed the expurgation, of course, because he usually stands with the players, even as he does the company's bidding. Yet, he pointed out that children would view inclusion of the words as endorsement of their use. And while tournament players could see the words as mere game pieces, the public was not able to separate words from their meanings. The bottom line? MB was not comfortable with the words, although only a few months earlier its president, E. David Wilson, didn't have a problem with them when he wrote to Judith Grad. Still, Williams wrote that the company wanted more people to play and the word tradeoff would further that goal. Then disingenuously transforming himself from a representative of the company to "just one of the players," Williams wrote, "Remember, the Scrabble game is their game [meaning the company's], even though those of us who are passionate about it think of it as ours."

The player response was overwhelmingly negative. Lester Schonbrun of California remembers it as the only issue that ever united tournament players, while New Mexico's Mike Baron recalls it as the most controversial issue ever to hit the game. Most serious players did think of it as their game and they didn't want anyone tinkering with the lexicon. In particular, they didn't like the idea of outside meddling, being bullied by Hasbro and MB, or that the company was in control of the lexicographical future of their game. It was a not-so-subtle reminder that they played organized Scrabble at the pleasure of the trademark holder, who could change the words, the rules, or whatever else it wanted, when it wanted, even though it had done little for the game other than buy it. And maybe that was, in part, at the root of the many protests that followed.

Numerous letters were fired off to management, but it was Paula Kaufman and Hilda Siegel of Boston who decided to do something on a larger scale. As Kaufman remembers it, she composed a protest letter that she showed to players at various Boston area clubs. Soon she was hooked up with Siegel, who wanted to take it further. The letter became a petition.

Siegel contacted John Williams at the NSA, but says that the man who would later say that he threatened to quit over the issue, didn't give her any encouragement. According to Siegel, Williams said, "Well, if I wanted to, I could go ahead." A rather tepid response, according to Siegel, particularly from someone who "felt passionately" about the game. So she bought a list of Scrabble club directors' names and addresses from the NSA (no waiving of fees for good causes here) and got started. It took about a month and cost Siegel a hundred dollars. "I was working against time," she says, "because they wanted to change the dictionary quickly." She sent the petition to clubs throughout the country.

Robin Levin of the San Francisco club circulated a petition. She says that virtually all players opposed expurgation. She remembers there was even talk, which didn't go very far, of starting an alternative players' organization. She fondly recalls Steve Alexander's bumper sticker that proclaimed, "I refuse to play

Scrabble with a child's dictionary." No doubt similar reactions took place across the country.

Not everyone opposed expurgation, however. When Jim Pate, a club director in Birmingham, Alabama, received Siegel's petition, he decided to circulate his own counter petition that supported removal of the words. Pate saw the expurgation as a business decision "based on certain ethical principles" and not censorship. It didn't bother him. In fact, he thought Scrabble would be a better game without the offending words. At least two top players, Jim Kramer of Minnesota and the late Bob Felt, of San Francisco, agreed with him.

Felt, who won the National Scrabble Championship in 1990, had broached the subject of removing offensive words in a town meeting held in conjunction with the Atlanta Nationals in 1992. He recalled getting hooted down. "My belief," said Felt, "is that the future of Scrabble is in the public schools and one way to get there is to use a purged word source." Kramer saw offensive terms as just another class of words that wouldn't be allowed, like OUI or IRAQ. "We needn't bury our heads and pretend that FUCKER is not a word," wrote Kramer, "we can just say that like OUI, IRAQ, and others, it's a word that isn't allowable in Scrabble."

While Hilda Siegel collected her 1000 signatures and Jim Pate his twenty or thirty, the NSA and MB were also at work. According to John Williams, who received anonymous obscene letters and threats, along with general derision from the players for being the company's lackey in this episode, he, Joe Edley, company attorneys, and Merriam-Webster editors set about compiling a list of words. (It should be noted that Jim Lowe at Merriam-

Webster would later say that he and his organization had nothing to do with it.) Williams says that he appealed to E. David Wilson, president of MB, for some sort of compromise. But, says Williams, playing the fear card he has become known for, "What I didn't want to do was alienate MB to the point they shut down the NSA. I also considered resigning, I felt so strongly about it." Indeed.

The expurgation controversy dragged on into the summer of 1994. At the time of the National Scrabble Championship held August 13 to 18 in Hollywood, California, the issue still simmered. Then Williams stepped to the microphone to announce a compromise, one that he claims as his own. The 100 or so offensive words would be deleted from the OSPD3, but there would be a separate word source, the *Official Club and Tournament Word List* (OWL), available only to NSA members, which would be used for club and tournament play.

The OWL solution satisfied just about everyone. The ADL was happy because the offending words would no longer corrupt young minds, unless they belonged to the NSA. Judith Grad and Hilda Siegel were happy because they both felt that they had had an impact. Hasbro execs were no doubt happy because by not taking a principled stand, the company had avoided what could have been a very ugly run-in with the ADL. Even Bob Felt was vindicated because his worst fears had been realized: the organized game lost its dictionary and ended up with a word list. As for Jim Pate, it wasn't quite the expurgation he had expected. The 50 to 100 offensive words had ballooned to about 200, prompting Pate to remark, "I probably would have removed only one third to one fourth as many words." Perhaps this proves that it takes a corporate lawyer to determine what constitutes true offensiveness. In the end, it was OSPD3 for the impressionable masses and OWL for serious players and has been ever since.

A consequence no one anticipated occurred a decade later. The ESPN cable network offered to televise several tournaments. What to do? Although there was much discontent among the players, the NSA announced that the expurgated word list would be used for the finals (but not for the rest of the tournament). It was implied that this was because of the FCC regulations. Of course, the FCC does not regulate cable stations, as anyone who has watched *The Sopranos* or *Deadwood* can testify. But what the heck, the players felt it was a small price to pay to get serious Scrabble in front of the general public.

At the 2004 Nationals this censorship came home to roost. During taping of the finals, the eventual winner, Trey Wright, played LEZ, one of the taboo words. Not to worry. It was spotted, the censors conferred, the tiles were picked up, and Wright made an alternative play. Thanks to the marvels of video editing the viewing public never realized this happened. Saved again.

This was followed in 2005 by expurgations that no one could have anticipated in 1994. New editions of the OSPD source dictionaries necessitated a revision of OSPD3. The product, OSPD4, contained some 3500 new words. Naturally, new offensive words such as POO were removed, but there was a new class of verboten words— product names and trademarked words. Words such as BRILLO, JELLO, BENADRYL, DUMPSTER, and about 100 more are now acceptable in club and tournament play, but not for the parlor player.

The parlor player was also saved from exposure to the

Trey Wright, on closed circuit screen, is on his way to winning the 2004 Nationals in New Orleans. Commentators are 13-year-old Andre Ornish, Robin Daniel, Chris Cree (back to camera), and Joel Sherman, standing far right. Facing the stage is Andre's father.

expurgated words in Mike Baron's recently published *Scrabble Wordbook*. Originally self-published in 1988 as *The Wordbook*, Baron began his quest for the Scrabble imprimatur in 1990. In 2007 he got it, but at a price. He had to agree to expurgating offensive words from his book of word lists. For those who come to his book signings, however, he provides a bookmark that contains what he calls "the poo list"—some two hundred fifty expurgated words from ABO to WETBACK.

There's more. Franklin Electronics has sold the electronic version of the OSPD since the early 1990s. The first post-expurgation Franklin device did not include the forbidden words. In 2008, however, it was announced that the latest dictionary would include both OSPD4 for the public and OWL2 for club and tournament players. OWL2, with its forbidden words, would only be available to NSA members who would receive a password at the time of their Franklin purchase.

I doubt that we have heard the last from Judith Grad.

No discussion of the lexicon would be complete without mentioning the dictionary that almost was. This dictionary—actually a word list—is used in most countries outside of North America, and may one day be adopted here. It's called SOWPODS. (Recently, Mattel/Spear, which owns the rights to Scrabble outside of North America, changed its word source. So SOWPODS has become *Collins Scrabble Words*.)

SOWPODS is an acronym for the combined British *Official Scrabble Words* (OSW) taken from *Chamber's Dictionary*, and the North American *Official Scrabble Players Dictionary* (OSPD). According to Graeme Thomas, former head of the Association of British Scrabble Players, SOWPODS gained favor in 1991 at the first World Scrabble Championship. For that event the two word sources were combined; in theory this leveled the playing field for participants from around the world, since they used either OSW or OSPD in everyday play. But more importantly, it equalized the lexicon for players from North America and the United Kingdom—the world's hotbeds of English language Scrabble.

Since 1991 some North American players have argued that SOWPODS should be the official word source in North America. An opposing group of players has resisted the conversion. Most rank and file club players knew little about the matter until the middle of 2000 when they were asked to vote on it.

SOWPODS would add about 30,000 words to the North American lexicon of roughly 100,000 words. Just the mention of some of those words—CH, EE, ZO, and YU, for example—is enough to raise the hackles of players dedicated to the defense of the *OSPD*. Still, *SOWPODS* is used in Australia, New Zealand, some African countries, Malaysia, Singapore, the Philippines, Sri Lanka, and the U.K. It's spreading, while the *OSPD* and its successor *OWL* (which contains the offensive words), is limited to North America, Israel, Malta, and Thailand. The pros and cons of *SOWPODS* shake out like this.

The PODSERS, as they are called, like to focus on the unification that would occur if everyone converted to *SOWPODS*. It would mean, they argue, that anyone who played English language Scrabble could sit down anywhere in the world and play with a common word source. This is referred to as "one Scrabble world." They also argue that *SOWPODS* will improve the game. Canada's Joel Wapnick, the 1999 World champion, says *SOWPODS* "requires greater tactical ability and strategic insight." Bob Lipton, a Florida player, has further noted that it enables players to come from behind more readily than they can with the *OSPD*. Words like ZO increase scoring opportunities, while some of the other unusual two letter words make it easier to develop overlapping plays and to attach high scoring seven-letter words to words that are already on the board. Total scores tend to be a bit higher and fewer racks are so bad that they must be exchanged. All pluses.

The resistance isn't convinced. Many are afraid of a

schism in North American play. Steve Oliger, of the Exton, Pennsylvania, club, fears that the growing interest in SOW- PODS will lead to SOWPODS tournaments, separate SOW- PODS divisions within OSPD tournaments, and a split in the NSA. They object to some of the unusual OSW words as essentially non-words. For example, they oppose the inclusion of obsolete English usages from Spenser and Chaucer, as well as words from the days before dictionaries created standardized spellings. They feel the obscure words will frighten off club players. They also worry about keeping the players the game already has: a few have said they will drop out if SOWPODS is adopted.

The debate is deadly serious. Postings on the topic on Crossword-Game-Pro, the Scrabble electronic listserv, has singed more than a few feathers. When Cheryl Cadieux, a Michigan player, made fun of SOWPODS, calling it WOS- DOPS, PODSERS were infuriated. Both she and Jim Miller, of California, took considerable flak for their comments. Then Miller started his own electronic list, where no one was allowed to discuss SOWPODS. Apparently he wasn't the only one sick of the debate, because it wasn't long before his subscribers jumped to well over 200.

Some saw the World Championship as the root of the problem. On the one hand it's the most prestigious event in Scrabble, but because of it some twenty or thirty North American players who aspire to the World's team must study SOWPODS words. Jim Miller sees no reason to turn North American Scrabble upside down to make it more convenient for these elite players. Steve Oliger has even said that he would rather see Hasbro junk the Worlds (recently it has, but Americans still participate). In other words, the anti-PODSERS consider the issue an elitist plot to make life easier for those who want to play in the Worlds, where they are wined and dined by the owners.

In 1999 the NSA announced there would be a *SOWPODS* vote in 2000. A victory of sorts for the *SOWPODS* camp. The *Scrabble News* laid out the pros and cons and clubs throughout North America were urged to have their members play *SOWPODS* games during *SOWPODS* month. Some clubs did, while most didn't. When the votes came in, the PODSERS had lost, but had done better than many had expected by getting some thirty-five percent of the ballots cast (less than half the membership participated). This means that the *OSPD* and its successor, *OWL*, still rule in North America. But there is talk of another vote, maybe in a few years.

What is interesting about the expurgation and *SOW-PODS* issues is the way they were handled by the company. In the case of expurgation, where real money was at stake, Hasbro imposed a solution on the letterati despite considerable protest. In the second case, where *SOWPODS* had no bottom line implications, the decision was left up to the players: a little participatory democracy to give the letterati the illusion of control. It also mollified some of the top players who have been pushing *SOWPODS* for years. The vote ended the carping with zero chance of a *SOWPODS* victory, so for the NSA, it was a win-win situation.

6

The Measure of a Player

The Rating System

When two Scrabble players meet they don't ask, "What is your sign?" They ask, "What is your rating?" Well, maybe not immediately, but one way or another the conversation will get around to it. That's because a rating establishes a player's status in the Scrabble hierarchy. It shows how much progress she has made and how far she has to go. It also tells a fellow player how hard she is trying and roughly what to expect if they decide to play.

Ratings didn't always convey a lot of information about a player. In 1973, when organized Scrabble began, there were no ratings. In fact, most people were unrated until 1984. Now, whatever players think of ratings, they take them as a given. Everyone who plays in tournaments is rated.

In simplified form, here is how it works. A player starts his tournament career unrated. In most cases this means playing in the bottom division of his first event. Most of his opponents will be rated. How he does against them will determine the rating he will receive once the NSA totals up the results of the tournament. The novice receives a few rating points for each game he wins and loses a few for each defeat. Once rated, if he accumulates wins over higher-ranked players his rating will rise. Ratings range from about 500 to 2000, with close to 3000 players rated. Roughly 500 are rated over 1500, with a handful rated more than 1900. It's not easy to get to the top.

In the 1970s and early 1980s, prior to ratings, Scrabble prowess was determined by "expert points." These points were amassed by winning games at local clubs and at tournaments. "Each win at a club or a tournament," according to Stu Goldman, "was worth one point." The totals were forwarded by club directors to SCGP and the points were periodically posted in the *Scrabble Players Newspaper*.

As of October 31, 1978, there were 191 expert players. They came in three classes: B (50–499 points), C (500–749 points), and D (750–1499 points). Only Stu Goldman, with 909 points, had made it to the D level. Goldman ran Long Island's Club No. 5, and played in eleven other clubs. "I may have played in as many as six a week," he says.

This system was better than nothing, but whether it measured skill or frequency of play was open to debate. In the late 1970s there were four or five alternate rating concepts kicking around. Then Dan Pratt decided to do more than talk about it. He was both a chess and Scrabble player and had a background in mathematics. He understood the math that underpinned the Elo rating system used by the United States Chess Federation.

In 1980, Jim Houle, who ran SCGP, told Pratt that it

would take many years worth of Scrabble tournament results before a rating system was possible. "I thought that was nonsensical," says Pratt, "and so Jim agreed to supply me with the results of that year's North American Invitational Championship and the regional tournaments that had served as qualifying events."

Pratt adapted the Elo system to Houle's data and some supplied by Mike Wise, Ron Tiekert, and Ted Rosen. Pratt's first pass at the problem produced a system with an average rating of 2000 for the 1980 Invitational participants, with a high of 2400. The system did not predict who would beat whom very well, says Pratt, "so after some thought and probably a few more tournaments I simply scrunched everyone's rating so that it would be two-thirds closer to 2000 than it had been." That made 2100 the top and resulted in more reliable predictions of wins and losses.

By 1982 Pratt had rated some 200 players on a sheet he called "The Rating Beadroll." He gave it to anyone who asked. Pratt had done his calculations by hand. This tedium, as well as the fact that he never wanted to do anything but prove a rating system was possible, led him to pass the torch to Charlie Southwell, a Northern Virginia player who did more tweaking of the system. In issue number 51 of the *Scrabble Players Newspaper* he gave the letterati their first peek at ratings by quantifying the relative strengths of the thirty-two competitors at the 1983 North American Championships in Chicago. The membership liked what it saw.

That presented a problem. Everyone wanted to be rated. This required more commitment of time than Southwell could afford. So late in 1982 he turned over a handwritten list of names and ratings, roughly 200, to

Stan Rubinsky and Mike Baron at the 1983 North American Invitational in Chicago. It's unclear who was consoling whom on a loss before the break between rounds on day 2. Mike's shirt is subtitled, "Society for the preservation of equal rights for men."

Alan Frank, who was really Scrabble's first ratings czar. Frank, a Boston area programmer, wrote software to do the ratings calculations. He then began to input tournament results from around the country and by early 1983 had rated 1200 players. He, too, tweaked the system.

The adjustments were again borrowed from the United States Chess Federation, says Frank, and were meant to enable underrated players to rise more quickly, high-rated players to avoid being penalized when they competed against lower-rated players and, in general, to reduce the natural tendency for ratings to deflate in any system that has a steady influx of new players.

Alan Frank takes the stage in Reno to get his tenth-place
finish money at the 1988 Nationals.

Frank treated the ratings as a business, charging a
dollar for each one he calculated. By late 1986 he had
rated some 3600 players. To celebrate the accomplishment
and show the letterati where they stood in comparison to
players nationwide, SCGP devoted most of the
October/November issue of *Scrabble Players Newspaper*
to ratings—including a twelve-page list of all 3600 players
from Elspeth Abbate (1600) to Pam Zvonac (1400). By
1991 there were 7000 rated players and the NSA offered to
buy Frank's business. Looking back on it, Frank feels that
he had no choice but to sell. He proposed a price. They
accepted. Today he says, "I didn't like the coerciveness of
it and I think they were annoyed at having to pay." This
brought the ratings under NSA control.

Ratings gave players a sense of how they stacked up
nationally and whether they were improving. Ratings also

permitted tournament directors to stratify events so players of similar ability could play against one another. This allowed players in each division to win prizes.

Bruce D'Ambrosio, who played before and after ratings, thinks it was the biggest change to ever hit organized Scrabble. He remembers the one-large-group period as a time when people paid anywhere from nothing to ten dollars to enter events and were happy to win a plaque or certificate. When ratings came along, says D'Ambrosio, it became easier to draw people to tournaments because more people felt they had a chance of winning something. The larger turnouts produced more entry fees, which bumped up the prize money pool and further increased the allure of tournaments.

There were division-based tournaments before 1984 but it was not common. The February 1982 issue of *Scrabble Players Newspaper* gave guidelines for creating divisions. Expert players were those with club averages above 350, intermediates were below 350, and novices had no previous tournament experience. Some tournaments were defined as "open," which meant there were no divisional restrictions. Things were much more amorphous before ratings.

The rating system did not prove to be problem-free. Despite the tweaking by Frank and others, some of the top players suspected that it did not always serve them well. The ratings formula used differences in ratings between players to predict how often the higher-rated player should win. But it didn't account for the luck factor in drawing tiles.

Every Scrabble player has to face the luck factor. Beginning players think they will lose to better players and triumph over weaker ones. As they gain experience they begin to understand that some of the time something else is going on. There are good tiles and bad tiles and a player will sometimes draw more of one than the other. There are also occasions when the tiles that come up match the words that a player knows. Or the board develops in such a way that it perfectly accommodates one player's tiles, but not his opponent's. The game becomes effortless. This is all part of the luck factor. Because of the luck factor, players will sometimes win when a ratings disparity indicates their chances are slim. Or they will lose when they are heavy favorites.

Jerry Lerman, a mathematically inclined California player, took a look at this phenomenon in 1992. Lerman knew that the top players had gotten better since the inception of the rating system in 1984, yet they were still rated around 2100. If the top players really were better, this meant that more skill levels were packed into the same range of ratings, which would undermine the system's ability to predict how often a higher-rated player would beat a lower-rated player. The more good players in the system, the worse the problem.

Lerman analyzed the results of 826 tournament games between expert players and discovered that ratings were effectively capped for top players because they could not meet the expectations of the system. He proposed changes that would conform more closely with reality.

That was fifteen years ago and the problem has probably gotten worse. That's because players have continued to get better and the number of top players has increased. Despite the best efforts of an NSA Ratings Committee to reform it and a Ph.D. dissertation in mathematics, by

Robert Parker at the University of New Mexico, aimed at replacing it, the system remains unchanged. According to Dan Stock, a professor of mathematics, and past chair of the Ratings Committee, "There are no perfect rating systems." This doesn't mean this is as good as it gets, but tweaks like building in a "luck factor" just don't work, says Stock.

In the meantime the rating system has a number of real world implications. People who have worked for years to build up their ratings want to protect them. According to Mike Baron, "Many are choosy about what events they go to, because they know the risk-to-gain ratio is very unfriendly to them." The obvious thing for high flyers to do is to avoid tournaments where weak, but possibly lucky, players might topple them and cause their ratings to plummet.

But it's not just the cream of the letterati who worry about ratings. Many lower-level players have a great deal of ego invested in their ratings. Dan Stock says they have found ways of manipulating the system to protect themselves. The most obvious strategy is to avoid tournaments where they will be the highest, or close to the highest, rated player in their divisions. Mike Baron describes an unusual variant of that technique. He and Mark Powell showed up at the 1990 Durango, Colorado, tournament to find that the advertised divisional ratings cutoffs would not be followed. Tourney organizers were allowing many lesser lights (which translated to potential rating busters) to play up in the expert division. "Mark Powell and I chose to sit out," says Baron. "We had a great two-player unrated tournament." After the tournament, Baron proposed that players have a rating within 100 points of a divisional cutoff before being allowed to "play up." The NSA adopted this proposal.

Some players are obsessed with ratings and constantly scheme and grumble about them, while the majority view them more as measuring sticks of their progress, and not as integral parts of their beings. Some calculate every tournament appearance in terms of getting that ratings bump, and there are others who will play anyone, anytime, anywhere. Take Ira Cohen, a California player, who is usually in the top one percent of the letterati. In late 1999, Cohen, an electrical contractor, took his 1900-plus rating to Newport, California, to an event run by Gary Moss. Surprisingly, he was rated several hundred points higher than anyone else in his division. Time to sit out, right? Wrong! Cohen was ready to play. Moss, however, didn't think it was fair. In fact, he had tried to contact Cohen the previous week to tell him to stay home. Moss says a friend passed the word along. Cohen said he never got it. On the day of the event, with Cohen in the wings, Moss polled several prospective opponents. They said they would sit out if Cohen played. "So I stood firm and didn't let him play," says Moss. An upset Cohen went home. Yet another outcome that the rating system doesn't predict.

CHAPTER

7

Let the Competition Begin

Early Tournaments

Scrabble players are always eager to find out who is the best. Nowhere is this more evident than in Scrabble's elaborate network of 200-plus tournaments. Just about every weekend there is at least one event, usually more, somewhere in North America. The letterati who take part are at the heart of the organized game. They are always trying to improve, and back at their clubs they push other players to get better too. But tournaments weren't always so commonplace.

Probably the first one was held in Reno, Nevada, in 1958 or 1959. Al Demers, the man who organized it, isn't quite sure. He was president of the Reno Chamber of Commerce at the time, and was able to get a number of businesses involved—for example, various casinos contributed liquor and prizes. Scrabble was very popular among intellectuals in the 1950s, so Demers advertised at universities throughout California and had a turnout of close to 500 for his event, held at Harold's Club. There was a smattering of students, along with a large contingent of faculty, says Demers. The entry fee was two dollars. It was an elimination format, which meant one loss and you went home. Demers doesn't recall how many games were played, but it must have been seven or eight, to eventually arrive at the last man standing. That man was Demers, who won a free weekend a month at Harrah's in Lake Tahoe—a year's worth. The second place finisher received $500. "We didn't know what we were doing," says Demers, "but it worked." He didn't do it again, though. "It was too much trouble," he says.

There were some unsanctioned events at the New York City chess clubs in the 1960s too, but it wasn't until 1973 in Brooklyn that sanctioned tournament Scrabble began. Co-sponsored by Scrabble Crossword Game Players Inc. (SCGP) and the New York City Department of Parks and Recreation, the first event was huge by today's standards. It ran from March 18 through April 15 under the direction of the late Joel Skolnick, of the Brooklyn borough office of the Parks and Recreation Department, who ran many subsequent events.

Ads for the tournament appeared in the *New York Times* next to the crossword puzzle. They attracted some 500, mostly New Yorkers, who competed on four consecutive Sundays. They played three fifty-minute games each weekend, used sand timers, had two minutes for each move, and used an elimination format. Steve Tier, of Queens, remembers that there were arguments over the accuracy of the sand timers—did they contain exactly two minutes worth of sand? The format was total points scored over the three games. The winner of each game received an additional fifty points to ensure there would be no collusion (in theory two players would not collude to amass astronomical scores if the winner received an additional fifty points). Ten finalists from each weekend slugged it out for the title. The winner was twenty-seven-year-old Jonathan Hatch, a musician and singer, who won a $100 Savings Bond and a certificate from the city. He also met Lee Tiffany, head of SCGP for Selchow & Righter.

Tiffany offered Hatch and his girlfriend, Kathy Flaherty (now his wife), the opportunity to promote Scrabble. "Once I simultaneously played ten or twelve people on boards set up at the World Trade Center," says Hatch. In the summer of 1973 he and Flaherty set up impromptu tournaments in the Catskills at Grosingers and the Concord Hotel. "I still have a steamer trunk full of boards from back then," he says.

In 1973 a thirteen-week event drew some 2000 players when contestants from all of the New York boroughs turned out to determine the New York champ. The field was eventually winnowed down to twelve finalists, from which Bernard Wishengrad emerged victorious. Five of these players went on to represent the city in a team match against Baltimore later that year. The New York players were Bill Greenberg, Francis Koestler, Jonathan Hatch, David Prinz and Ron Tiekert, although Tiekert was unable to make the trip. They went up against Gordon Shapiro, Dan Pratt, John Jarowski, Al Schector, and Ron Holmes, and lost twelve of the twenty games to the Baltimore tile pushers. "We won," says Shapiro, "but it was because Ron Tierkert couldn't come and all of his games were forfeited."

There were events in Brooklyn well into the 1980s, says Stu Goldman, who took part in a number of them. Goldman, who had played serious Scrabble at the Game Room and other chess clubs in Manhattan, remembers the Parks and Recreation events well. About 100 people would gather at the Brooklyn War Memorial Recreation Center in Codman Plaza Park each Sunday, says Goldman. The initial pairings for the event were ostensibly random. Participants sat where they pleased, at long tables, then played the person seated across from them. Each player rotated one seat to her right for the following game. Goldman says none of the experienced players from the chess clubs wanted to mix it up with a tough opponent at the start, so a rule of thumb developed. "Find three players in a row studying the two-letter word list as though their lives depended on it," says Goldman, "and sit opposite the one on the left."

That's roughly how Paul Avrin, who was a Game Room regular, remembers it. "What you wanted to do," says Avrin, who is a retired math teacher, "was to stay away from any face you recognized, or at least be on the same side of the table with them." Turnout for the 1970s Brooklyn events was in the thousands, but dwindled to a few hundred in the 1980s. "As the general public began to realize they were up against people who had Scrabble skills," says Goldman, "the sucker ranks began to thin out."

Selchow & Righter learned a lot from the Brooklyn events. The most important lesson: the potential afforded by the nationwide web of parks and recreation departments. The company sent representatives to the Congress for Recreation and Parks, a convention sponsored by the

The quarter finals of the 1979 New York City Tournament.
Steve Pfeiffer (R) checking out Paul Avrin's moves at the
next board. Directly behind Avrin is future U.S., Canadian,
and World champion Joel Wapnick.

National Recreation and Park Association. Recreation departments around the country were soon co-sponsoring events with Scrabble Crossword Game Players Inc. The *Scrabble Players Newspaper* told members to contact their local parks and recreation departments if they wanted to put on a tournament. According to Jim Houle, who ran SCGP from 1976 to 1985, Selchow & Righter provided the equipment in the early years. Boards, tiles, racks, and score sheets were sent back and forth between national headquarters and tournament directors on a regular basis. "We even fixed broken sets," says Houle.

In 1975, events were held in Memphis, Tennessee, Mobile, Alabama, Dallas, Texas, and Suffolk County, New York. During this same period, Charles Goldstein, who played in the first North American Invitational in 1978, recalls events in Sacramento, Oakland, and San Jose, California. "They were considered the big California tournaments," says Goldstein. There was also a large event in Miami, Florida, according to Steve Polatnick, who played in it for many years. It began in the mid 1970s, says Polatnick, and "was a mob scene" very similar to the early Brooklyn tournaments after which it was modeled.

Some events didn't fit the mold. Club Mensa, the high IQ group, co-sponsored several in Miami, as did Northwestern University in Chicago and the University of Michigan in Ann Arbor. Ron Tiekert, who would go on to win the 1985 Nationals, remembers that in the mid 1970s the late Milt Wertheimer put on four round-robin events at Nathan's Famous, a restaurant in Manhattan known for its hot dogs, French fries, and hamburgers.

Until someone says otherwise, the award for the first weekend tournament, without the help of the local department of parks and recreation, goes to Club No. 8 in Yonkers, New York. The event took place at the Hotel Brickman in South Fallsberg, New York, from September 30 through October 2, 1977. It was organized for club members, according to the *Scrabble Players Newspaper*, but soon mushroomed into a happening that attracted seventy-eight players from New York, New Jersey, Connecticut, and Pennsylvania.

Bernie Teitelbaum of Yonkers ran it, Barry Patten won it, and Ann Sanfedele recalls having a great time. She says, "After the tourney the three of us [she, Barry Patten, and Steve Tier] threw a set of tiles into the pool and literally fished for bingos." Scrabble Crossword Game Players Inc. reported on the tournament but didn't make much of this first-time event, which quickly spread to other clubs and broke the Parks and Recreation co-sponsorship template that had been in place since 1973.

With tournaments sprouting up across North America and the *Scrabble Players Newspaper* reporting on them, it wasn't long before people wanted to know who was the most accomplished player in the land. It fell to SCGP to find out. From May 19 to 26, 1978, all Scrabble eyes were on Loews Summit Hotel in New York City, where sixty-four competitors and eight alternates gathered for the first North American Invitational. They came from fourteen states and Canada. The event was by invitation only.

Jim Houle, who headed up SCGP, consulted club directors to determine who would get the invites. Dan Pratt, who placed second in the tournament, says, "The basic criterion was to get the best players from every part of North America." But there was a hidden agenda. Selchow & Righter wanted to get publicity in as many places as possible. This became clear when many of the Midwestern players proved to be less than formidable opponents and New York players or former New Yorkers swept twelve of the top positions in the tournament.

There was a second way to get invited, says Shazzi Felstein, who played in the event. Some players were picked because Mike Senkiewicz, S&R's in-house expert, thought that they were good. Felstein should know; she was Mike's significant other at the time. She was also one of Mike's "at-large" selections, which she says irked a lot of people. "Many players thought I was invited because I was Mike's girlfriend," she says. "Fortunately, I finished ninth and that shut everyone up."

Felstein and Senkiewicz weren't the only ones associated

Foreground, Shazzi Felstein ponders a move at the North
American Invitational in 1978. Barry Patten is in the background.

with the event who had family ties. Carol Skolnick (now
Carol Felstein Vignet), the word judge, was Shazzi's sister.
And Carol's husband was Joel Skolnick, the tournament

director. That made Senkiewicz his de facto brother-in-law, which was the way he was often introduced. New York's Scrabble elite was a tight-knit group.

The prizes were small, but it was the first time Scrabble players had competed for more than pocket change. There was $8400 in total, with $1500 going to the winner and a $1000 to the second place finisher. This was a bonanza to people used to vying for plaques and certificates. Jim Houle says he first proposed to the s&r board of directors that the first prize be $5000. So he inched downward until they reached agreement. "It was an experiment as far as they were concerned," says Houle, "but I saw it as a growing thing."

Steve Polatnick, of Miami (who along with Joel Wapnick of Montreal, Quebec, is the only player to have played in every national championship since 1978), recalls the excitement. He says Joel Skolnick was quite concerned about whether people would show up, and if they didn't, what he would do. Everyone came, though, and Polatnick remembers that on the first day of the event Skolnick recounted his fears to the assembled group. "At that moment," says Polatnick, "everyone experienced a spine tingling thrill because they knew we all loved the game and our attendance was proof of that."

The tournament used a credit system to determine the winner, rather than the total number of points scored, as had been done in the Brooklyn events, or the total number of games won, as has become the custom since 1980. "Under the credit system," says Pratt, "you got three points for winning. However, you also got one point for each fifty points by which you defeated your opponent, along with one point for each fifty points you scored." This system eventually came back to haunt Pratt.

According to Stu Goldman, almost from the start the system slowed down between rounds because determining who would play whom turned out to be more complicated than anyone had expected. "They had six guys with calculators doing the figuring," says Goldman. Pratt recalls that the waits between games were as much as an hour. On the second day, when an evening banquet was on tap, the last two games had to be scrapped so that everyone could arrive at the dinner on time, says Goldman. This made it a sixteen-game event instead of the advertised eighteen.

There were some other differences. Take going first. Pratt says that tiles were drawn every game to see who would start. Since the person who plays first is at a slight advantage, this could greatly work against someone who had a string of losing draws. It happened to Mike Wise of Ontario. "Mike Wise noted that he only went first once in the whole tournament," says Pratt, "and ever since we've had the system we are all familiar with" in which all players go first about half the time.

There were no shouts of "Challenge" or "Director." The rules stipulated: "Players entering challenges or seeking any other assistance will simply raise their hand without calling out." There were no temper tantrums or shenanigans, as sometimes occurs today. "Everyone was on their best behavior," says Polatnick.

Another difference was the time allotted for a game, twenty minutes instead of today's twenty-five, which put a premium on quick thinking. Challenges also had to be made quickly—within fifteen seconds or the right to challenge was forfeited. Today, players can deliberate as long as they like.

The players did not use preprinted tracking sheets to

check off the tiles as they were played, according to Pratt. Each player began the game with a blank sheet of paper for scorekeeping and some created a tracking sheet as they played. Ron Tiekert even objected to tracking. "You aren't allowed to write down the pip count in backgammon," says Tiekert, "nor can you do paper tracking of the cards played in bridge. So why should Scrabble be any different? All off-board activity should be mental, shouldn't it?"

No one was permitted to count or even see the pool of unplayed tiles, says Goldstein. Instead of residing in a tile bag as they do today, the tiles were face down in a box. Paul Avrin says the box top and bottom were taped together in an L-shape, so that the bottom could hold the tiles and the top could serve as a barrier to prying eyes. They used the box approach, says Goldstein, "because people were afraid of brailing" the wooden tile surfaces to locate the blanks.

Tiekert says there was also a problem with phony blanks. The tiles were supposed to start out face down in the box, although the players could not be certain of that because the tiles were behind the cardboard barrier. After drawing, the players turned the tiles face up on their racks. But mistakes happen, and not all the tiles started their trip from box to rack face down. So some players flipped their tiles from front to back, found a blank surface, thought they had blanks, and played them as such. "I played one myself," says Tiekert.

Chess clocks were new to the game, says Pratt. Jean Carol of Ohio, who had never seen one, was paired with Steve Williams of New York City, who had, but liked to play fast. Apparently Carol just followed Williams' lead because "everyone thought something had gone wrong," says Pratt, "when they got up and left while we were still playing." They had finished their game in a total of seven minutes.

The eventual winner was David Prinz of San Francisco, who was originally a New York player who had made it to the finals of the 1974 New York City championship. Prinz is a story himself. He hadn't played competitively since 1976, but along with Jonathan Hatch and Kathy Flaherty had just finished compiling the *Official Scrabble Players Dictionary*. During this period he was also Selchow & Righter's expert witness in a lawsuit brought by player Mark Landsberg. Since Prinz hadn't been playing tournaments, he wasn't even invited to the event, he says. "I was in good shape, though, because I had just written the dictionary," he says.

He called Jim Houle and asked for an invite. Houle said no. Prinz told him he ought to check with S&R's legal department. How was it going to look if their expert witness in a million-dollar lawsuit didn't play? "An hour later he called me back," says Prinz, "and said, 'You're invited.'"

After round nine Prinz was in tenth place. Then he was matched with New Yorker Josh Silber and everything turned around. Not far into the game Silber played HOME-FIRE, which got challenged off with a loss of turn. Prinz followed with TONSURE, which Silber incorrectly challenged. Another lost turn. A play or two later Prinz combined FLINDER with TONSURE to make TONSURED. Silber challenged again. He lost another turn. By the end it was Prinz 553 to Silber's 245, the most lopsided score of the tournament. It catapulted Prinz into third place.

Although Dan Pratt finished 13–3, while Prinz was

The first North American Invitational in May 1978. Jim Houle
(L) reaches out a hand to congratulate winner David Prinze
(R). Joel Skolnick, tournament director, looks on.

just 10–6, under the credit system Prinz had accumulated
173 points to Pratt's 170. In fact, seven players had
better win/loss records than Prinz, but the only thing that
mattered was the credit points. What still seems to irk
Pratt is that he was in first place and Prinz in second,
going into the final round. If that were the case today,
they would play each other, but not in 1978. There was
a rule prohibiting rematches, says Pratt. "I had already
beaten him handily."

It might have bothered Pratt even more if he knew how
Prinz approached his last game. Prinz was friendly with
Roz Grossman, who had to play Pratt. As Prinz recalls it,
he told her, "Shazzi Felstein is going to try to hold me

down, so see what you can do against Danny. Don't let him score. I'm begging you." Today, Grossman, who is in her late seventies and living in Israel, doesn't recall the particulars, but says, "David is probably right. Why would he make up a story like that?" The fact that the game was close and low scoring "was probably just coincidence," says Grossman. It meant that Pratt only picked up a few credits for the victory.

In the meantime Prinz demolished Felstein. She opened with AVERT, says Prinz, with the E on the star. Prinz had PELORIA (an abnormal regularity of a flower form) on his rack and knew that it combined with three other letters (N, S, T) to form eights. "There was the T and my heart just sang," recalls Prinz. He knew he had PETIOLAR (pertaining to a petiole). He played, she challenged and lost a turn. The game was a rout: Prinz 439, Felstein 290. Scrabble had its first national champion.

Befittingly, when Prinz stepped up to the podium at the post-tournament award ceremonies, one of the things he received along with his $1500 check, was the first copy of the *Official Scrabble Players Dictionary*, a volume he had just spent two and a half years compiling.

The Scrabble tournament circuit has come a long way since 1978, but it has a long way to go. Most tournaments are put on by clubs, and the events have increased at a more rapid rate than the number of people who want to play in them. Several thousand players compete each year where the average event draws fifty or sixty tile pushers. The limiting factors are time and money. Most players have a finite amount of both. Everyone who plays tournament Scrabble goes into the red to do so. They have to be selective.

Denver is a good example. When we had tournaments, some of us opened our homes to outside players; we provided homemade meals at the tournament site, and larger prizes than would have been expected (club members guaranteed them with their own money). In Calgary, Alberta, club member Siri Tillekeratne will pick up players at the airport, house them, and return them to the airport when a tournament is over. The Calgary club raises some $1500 each year from members through playing fees, which goes directly into their tournament fund. "Many club members also donate cash and material to be given away as door prizes at the tournament," says Tillekeratne.

Some tournaments are marathons of forty or fifty games over six days; some provide only seven games on a Sunday afternoon. In between, and much more common, are events with fourteen rounds played over a weekend. The main prizes, which are cash, come out of the entry fees. Many players argue that Scrabble is a serious competitive sport; prize money rewards excellence, shows respect for the game and will one day lead to a professional Scrabble tour, with stars, fame, and possibly fortune. Joel Sherman, of New York, says, "I would like to see it progress to the level that some people actually can support themselves by playing." The prize money, such as it is, plays a role in determining where many players choose to compete: the more prize money the better, even if it does little more than cover the expenses of the winner.

Entry fees run anywhere from $35 to $150. In theory, at least, quite a few people in each event have an opportunity to win something. Ron Tiekert's Game Room events in New York in the late 1970s had entry fees, but most tournaments didn't. It wasn't until 1981 that most events

"Show me the Money"—Ron Tiekert ran the Game Room
tournaments in the late '70s and early '80s. This photo was
taken in 1979; Ron is giving all the marbles to Merrill Kaitz.

began to charge, at first anywhere from $2 to $15. About
the same time, Tiekert jumped his fees to $22. Then came
the rating system, and tournaments could group players so
those with similar abilities played against one another.
Today most events have three or four divisions; a few have
six or seven. Each division has a winner and a number of
runners-up, all of whom receive prizes.

The letterati have tried various approaches to prize
money allocation, but given corporate constraints on tournament Scrabble there is no simple solution. The structure
of tournaments is left up to individual directors; previously, the trademark owner says they may not solicit outside sponsorship. But the 2007 Baltimore tournament was
sponsored by a bank, and the prize money was substan-
tial. Hasbro could sweeten the tournament purses, yet it

has never done so—even though the tournament and club structures serve to keep Scrabble in the news. The Scrabble that Hasbro seems to care about is played in living rooms across North America by people who wouldn't know a bingo stem from a flower stem. That's where the real money is.

Who's the Best?

The Nationals Evolve

Since the 1978 North American Invitational there have been face-offs every year or two to determine the best player in North America. Over the years the event has evolved, but has always provided good PR for first Selchow & Righter, then Hasbro, along with competition and spectacle for the players. Those who are new to tournament Scrabble, however, would find little resemblance between today's National Championship and many of its predecessors.

Change began with the name. In 1980, the North American Invitational became the North American Championship, which was held from November 14 to 16 at the Miramar-Sheraton Hotel in Santa Monica, California. The name change reflected a new approach to player selection. Instead of Jim Houle, head of SCGP, handpicking the players, as was largely the case in 1978, regional qualifying events were held throughout the United States and Canada.

The regionals took place in Baltimore, Chicago, Miami, San Francisco, Toronto, and New York City. Selchow & Righter got various retailers involved. The New York event was held at Macy's Department Store, while in Miami it was Jordan Marsh, in Chicago Kroch's and Brentano's bookstore, in San Francisco The Emporium, and in Toronto Simpsons. Sixty-four players vied for five spots in each of the American regionals, with four slots to Canada and three reserved for "wild card" entrants, players who had failed to qualify, but who had outstanding performances in their regionals. The result was a field of thirty-two, half the size of the group that played in 1978. Best of all, from the players' perspective, s&r picked up the tab to fly them to California.

Procedurally, Scrabble evolved too. The *Funk & Wagnalls College Dictionary*, as the official arbiter of organized play, was ushered out after the 1978 Invitational. It was replaced by the *Official Scrabble Players Dictionary* (*OSPD*), which removed most of the subjectivity from word judging. The tiles came out of the shielded box of 1978, and returned to the tile bag. The time allotted for a game also increased, jumping to twenty-two minutes from the twenty allotted in 1978, which encouraged tile tracking, says Charles Goldstein. Repeat matches were allowed; Dan Pratt, who finished fourth, considered that a modest improvement. The credit system was scrapped, so that never again would a national champion win fewer games than the second place finisher, as had happened in 1978.

Before the championship, Jim Houle met with the players, and during the meeting, the "Schonbrun courtesy rule" was born. Lester Schonbrun suggested that a player who might want to challenge a word should be given a minute to think about it and be able to put his opponent "on hold" while doing so, which meant that after thirty seconds the opponent could draw tiles, but not place them on his rack until the hold was lifted. Jim Pate says there were other discussions too, but the players soon tired of them and wanted to play. And they did.

When the first North American Championship was over, the headline in the *Scrabble Players Newspaper* read, "Night Watchman Is North American Champ." Joe Edley, who would go on to many other wins, was no average night watchman. He had scored 800 on his math SAT, had graduated from the University of Michigan, and was one of the first serious players of the game. He took the security job so that he could study at night. A wild card entrant, Edley emerged with a 14–3 record, to edge out New York City lawyer James Neuberger who was 13.5–3.5 for the title. Neuberger had gone into the last round with a half game lead and twice Edley's spread (the number of points by which he had beaten his previous opponents), which made for a cliffhanger finish, which Edley won 400 to 319 when he drew eight of the ten power tiles (the JQXZSSSS and two blanks). For his efforts he received $5000, up from the $1500 prize of 1978, and a trip to London.

There were fewer changes in 1983, when from August 10 to 12 the letterati met at the Drake Hotel in Chicago for yet another North American shootout. Again the total prize money crept higher, this time to $13,600. Four levels of qualifying rounds had been held in eight regions throughout the United States and Canada to determine the final thirty-two competitors. Goldstein recalls that playing in the North American Championship had become so important that people who failed to qualify in one regional often traveled to another part of the country to take a second crack at it. "If you could, you would," says Goldstein, who played in qualifiers in Albuquerque, San Diego, Los Angeles, and Phoenix. "At the time, the idea of missing a national Scrabble tournament was unthinkable," says Goldstein. Many familiar faces were back, including Joe Edley, Dan Pratt, Ron Tiekert, and Jim Neuberger.

There was a lot of PR. For the first time, the Nationals had a sponsor: Arby's, a restaurant chain. Chicago had a Scrabble Week, with special Scrabble events coordinated by the Chicago Parks and Recreation Department, Kroch's and Brentano's bookstore, and the Drake Hotel. Goldstein recalls a tile hunt on the beach at Lake Michigan. Selchow & Righter reps buried unusually colored tiles in the sand and encouraged kids to dig them up for prizes. A few of the players collected the tiles too, says Goldstein. "I still have some."

Goldstein, known in San Francisco Scrabble circles as "the villain," again made a unique statement. At a reception for the players and media, which included S&R execs and Scrabble inventor Alfred Butts, Goldstein showed up in a costume constructed from Scrabble boards. It had been put together by a professional costume designer in California. "I went to fittings and everything," says Goldstein. It was a boxy affair, which reached from head to toe and gave him a robot-like appearance. "Everyone thought it was a hoot and was in keeping with Charles' eccentric personality," says Chris Cree, who came up from Dallas to play.

The tournament itself took on yet another structure. Again it was the best of seventeen games, but this time a divisional component was added. Players competed in

The 1983 North American Championship in Chicago at the
Drake Hotel. Joel Wapnick smiles after having just defeated
Joe Edley to win the championship. Milt Wertheimer
annotated Wapnick's moves. Barbara Amster is in the
background with a TV crew that was recording the game.

groups of four during the first ten games. Then the top
eight players squared off in a seven-game round robin,
while the other twenty-four were assigned to three groups
of eight to compete for divisional titles. There was a 100-
point penalty for playing before writing down your opponent's score, for any scoring error, and for not writing
down the word that you played. The 100 points was subtracted from a player's cumulative point spread for the
tournament.

Joel Wapnick, a music professor from McGill University in Montreal, eventually pulled away from the pack

with a 13–4 record. He won $5000 and a trophy: a bronze "S" mounted on a travertine marble base. Not far behind was bridesmaid Dan Pratt at 12–5, who had finished second in 1978 and fourth in 1980.

In 1985 everything got bigger and better. In Boston there were more prizes, more contestants, and more rounds. The North American Scrabble Open was the largest sanctioned Scrabble tournament ever held, with 302 players, and $52,000 in prizes. The Open was held over four days from July 28 to 31; there were twenty-two games and the first prize was $10,000 and a trip for two to Hawaii. "It was the biggest NSC at that time, more games than ever, a small contingent of overseas players, and one big ballroom with all these tile shufflers," says Mike Baron. "Selchow & Righter was rolling in big bucks from sales of Trivial Pursuit in 1984," says Baron. "Subsidizing a grand event in 1985 was pocket change for them, and they got their two minute slot on *Good Morning America*, which is why they did it in the first place," he says. John Williams, who did PR work for S&R and now heads up the NSA, agrees. "The 1985 North American Open Scrabble Championship featured a hot sit-down lunch every day for 400 people, an opening and closing party, and all kinds of goodies," says Williams. "The total cost was upwards of $300,000."

Sponsors were everywhere. Arby's was back. At many of its locations across the country the public had been able to pick up inquiry cards to learn about the qualifying tournaments. There was also American Airlines, Merriam-Webster (publisher of the *Official Scrabble Players Dictionary*), and the Sheraton Hotel chain, which hosted the event in Boston. The front page of the *Scrabble Players*

Newspaper for February 1985 prominently displayed the logos of these companies, something that the Scrabble world would never see again. At the time, though, it must have seemed to many players that Scrabble was about to take off.

It was an "open" tournament, with no divisions, so anyone who wanted a chance at the brass ring had to be prepared to sit across the table from the best. Even though there was no entry fee for the 1985 Open, there wasn't much chance for most people to win any of the prize money. The prize fund had ballooned to a new high, but only the top thirty-two finishers, about 10% of the field, collected any of it. Still, for people used to tournaments with at most thirty or forty competitors, to see a room filled with 300 kindred souls, must have brought on more than a few goosebumps. The prize money? "I didn't give it a thought. It was just thrilling to be there," enthused Susan Moon, of Denver.

Computer pairing made its debut with an inauspicious glitch. Dan Pratt remembers that someone noticed that many of the top players were matched with one another right off the bat, something that usually didn't happen until well into the tournament. So the pairings had to be redone. It was between a one- and two-hour wait, says Mike Baron. What did people do? "Kvetch, until it was announced, 'Lunch is on the house,'" he says.

In the end, Ron Tiekert, a New York City children's book editor, finished first with a remarkable record of 20–2, with his only losses coming at the hands of Joe Edley and Jim Neuberger. He won $10,000, the largest amount of money ever awarded in Scrabble, plus the trip for two to Hawaii.

In 1987 players didn't have to win to have fun in the sun, they only had to show up, since the tournament was held in sunny Las Vegas. It was billed as "the Western Championship," but has since become known as the "substitute Nationals" because the real Nationals were never held. In 1986, Coleco Industries bought Selchow & Righter. It planned to hold the 1987 Nationals in July at the San Francisco Hyatt Regency, with two levels of qualifying rounds, and $60,000 in prize money, with the winner taking home $10,000. Scrabble Crossword Game Players Inc. expected some 300 players and encouraged international entries. Then the wheels came off.

According to John Williams, who had taken over for Jim Houle as editor and publisher of the SPN, "many changes were taking place with Scrabble." In his editorial in the June 1987 issue he explained that the future of SCGP, which had been up in the air at Coleco, was settled. It would continue, but with reduced funding. This meant that the 1987 North American Scrabble Open would be postponed. The announcement came just a month prior to the anticipated San Francisco event.

In the same issue of the newsletter, Joe Edley, the 1980 champ, and Johnny Nevarez, a strong player in his own right, announced the Western Championship, as a substitute for the defunct Nationals. It would be over the same dates, July 5 to 8, but at the Sahara Hotel and Casino in Las Vegas. They scheduled twenty-one games, promised $15,000 in prizes, $5000 to the winner, and no qualifying rounds. Surprisingly, it worked. People switched their plans at the last minute and showed up 326 strong.

It was a tight tournament to the end. With three rounds left to play, eight people had a chance to win it. One of

Rita Norr tracking tiles during a game at New York's Club No. 56 in 1988, less than a year after she won the 1987 "Unofficial" Nationals.

them was Jere Mead, a Massachusetts Latin teacher. Another was Rita Norr, a Brooklyn player with a Ph.D. in computer science. They both won their last games. This gave them 17–4 records, and Norr the victory and $5000, because she had won her 17 games by 81 more total points than Mead, who won $3000.

A sign of the times was that Norr's prize money was not easy to raise, according to John Williams. Coleco already showed signs of the financial problems that would put it out of business inside of two years. "It was increasingly clear that Coleco wouldn't or couldn't support the players," says Williams. "I had to beg for the money and the trip to Las Vegas."

In 1988 a still financially ailing Coleco tried again. The company didn't make the sort of commitment to the Nationals that S&R had in the past or that Milton Bradley would in the future, but it did underwrite most of the expenses and contribute $15,000 to the prize fund, with $5000 targeted to the winner. In retrospect this wasn't bad, considering that Coleco had serious money problems of its own. It went into chapter 11 bankruptcy in the spring of 1988 and tried to get back on its feet.

In spite of this, from July 31 to August 5, the 1988 National Scrabble Crossword Game Championship was held at the Sands Regency Hotel and Casino in Reno, Nevada. The Sands management put on a buffet reception for the players, co-sponsored with Coleco, and chipped in $3000 for the first- and $2000 for the second-place prizes. The tournament was wide open—players could just show up. But there was another new twist: the entry fee of $65. There had been one in 1987, but that was not an official trademark holder–sponsored event. It was put on by the players and they had to raise the prize money. It set a precedent that a financially strapped Coleco did not fail to notice. This started the entry fee practice that Hasbro has continued to this day. It didn't seem to affect turnout in 1988, since 323 tile pushers made the trek to Reno.

Following the lead of the 1987 Western Open, where Joe Edley and Johnny Nevarez had spread the prize money around much more than in past Nationals, the 1988 event spread it even further. It was the first Nationals to have

Foreground, Bob Schoenman at the 1988 Nationals in Reno.
Bob developed Protiles for tournament play. The blurry guy
on the left is Lester Schonbrun.

two divisions, where those rated over 1600 played in the
Expert Division, while everyone else duked it out in the
Recreational Division. The bulk of the prize money,
$14,650, still went to the experts, but $5250 also made its
way to the bottom dwellers. This marked a shift toward a
more egalitarian distribution of prizes, which would continue at future events.

Another tradition began in 1988. Bob Schoenman had
introduced Protiles in 1986, substitute plastic tiles, which
were smooth and not subject to brailing. For the 1988
Nationals he donated 160 sets in ivory white and bluish
gray, to keep everything on the up and up, and established
the Protile precedent that exists to this day.

Bob Watson (seated, left) has just defeated Joel Wapnick at the 1988 North American Championship in Reno. Tournament director Joe Edley looks over Bob's shoulder. Milt Wertheimer (center) was the annotater.

The 1988 Nationals were the only Nationals ever won by a physician: Dr. Robert Watson of Minneapolis. It's not likely to happen again, according to Watson, who retired from competitive Scrabble shortly after his victory. "The demands of medical practice in this age of exploding knowledge," says Watson, "are just too great." Watson could no longer find enough time for Scrabble, his family, and his job.

It wasn't obvious at the time, but the Nationals began to settle down in 1989. First, Coleco went belly-up, then Milton Bradley (MB), an arm of Hasbro, bought it out. Milton Bradley wasn't quite sure what to do with Scrabble Crossword Game Players. Its head, John Williams, who ran the organization through his PR and marketing firm, had to keep the group afloat with his own money for the better part of a year. Still, Hasbro and Williams have brought continuity to the Nationals.

In 1989 the event was held in the Pen Top Room at the Penta Hotel in New York City, where the letterati organized and paid for a modest reception, while MB chipped in for the prizes. Two hundred and twenty-one players entered the event. Peter Morris, who had finished second to Watson in 1988, beat Ron Tiekert in the last game to finish 21–6 to Tiekert's 20–7. It was a satisfying win for Morris, who, after coming so close in 1988, took home $5000.

Since 1989 Hasbro has put on nine Nationals without a major hitch and since 1991, in alternate years, has also cooperated with Spear/Mattel in the United Kingdom to put on a World Championship—although recently it has opted out of that arrangement, arguing that its market is North America, not the world. Still, in the United States, attendance at the Nationals has climbed from a low of 221 in New York in 1989 to a high of 837 in New Orleans, Louisiana, in 2004. Total prize money has risen from $25,000 in 1989 to $89,000 in 2004, while the 2004 winner Trey Wright walked away with $25,000.

Over the years the number of rounds has jumped from sixteen in 1978 to thirty-one, and some would like to see it go higher. The credit system of 1978 was scrapped, so since 1980 the champion has always been the player with the most wins. Since 1988 the prize money has increasingly trickled down through the ranks as the event has gone from two divisions in 1988 to three in 1994, four in 1996, and finally seven in 2004. It seems clear that as players at all levels have seen their chances of winning increase, more and more have chosen to give the Nationals a whirl.

The Nationals has become the premiere tournament in North American Scrabble. It has more players, prize money, and pomp and circumstance than any other event. It has become the game's primary PR happening too, which generates oodles of television, print media, and internet coverage for the game and Hasbro. It's a win-win situation for the letterati and the company.

9

Coming Out of the Parlor

The Club Scene

Over 200 Scrabble clubs are scattered across North America. They bear faint resemblance to the game rooms of New York in the 1960s. They are typically the cheapest, catch-as-catch-can venues that the financially strapped groups can find.

In Denver we meet in a church basement and at two bookstores. A quick perusal of the National Scrabble Association club list suggests that we are not alone. Churches, bookstores, recreation centers, senior centers, suburban clubhouses, restaurants, and banks are common meeting places. Some clubs are free. We charge $3 a night because we pay rent. In New York it's somewhat more.

Club members are typically serious, sometimes rabid players of the game. Many eat, sleep, and breathe Scrabble, often squeezing study and play into already busy schedules. In fact, it could be argued that what they lack in numbers, the letterati make up for with their intensity and enthusiasm. A dearth of serious players exists, though, despite the fact that 30 million American homes have Scrabble sets, and just about everyone who can read and write has played the game. Why haven't the clubs caught on?

For one, the game's owners have never done much to publicize the clubs. There isn't a list in every game box, on the inside cover of the Scrabble dictionary or at your local game shop. Only recently has such a roster made its way to the web.

Beyond that, most people have a lot going on in their lives. It's not that simple to make room for yet another activity, particularly one that requires an alert mind at the end of the day, when most people are ready to kick back. Then there is the misconception that what goes on at Scrabble clubs is essentially what happens at home. Some parlor players feel they already know how to play, have family and friends to play with, and couldn't get anything new from a club, except another entry in their day planners.

And then there are the people who want to play at clubs. First they have to conquer their fear of embarrassment. Scrabble, after all, is a battle of wits. No one likes the idea of losing, or in particular, losing in the public sort of way that one might envision at a club. A number of players have confided to me that it was this fear that kept them from coming. "I've been meaning to do this for a long time," they say, "but I had to work up my nerve."

Some never do. If ten percent of the people who inquire about our club by phone or e-mail actually came, our meetings would be overflowing. It's not uncommon for these prospects to bend my ear for fifteen or twenty minutes and then never make an appearance.

Those who do want to compete still have to clamber over the hurdle from parlor play. Many expect to play much as they do at home, where people eat, drink, talk, and might take two or more hours to finish a game. They may use open dictionaries and even have their own set of rules, says David Goodman, who directs the Albany, New York, club. Yet, there isn't much of that in club Scrabble. "Club Scrabble is not the same game," says Goodman.

Most clubs play tournament-style Scrabble, with little or no socializing during games. Talking, except in hushed tones, is frowned upon. There aren't many smiles. I often think of club Scrabble as the grim game. But for most newbies the seriousness is only part of the problem.

Parlor players often play three or four to a board. Not so at clubs, where it's always one-on-one. This means there's no one else to blame for a loss. One's intellectual self-worth is on the line. It's all the worse because most of these new players are accustomed to winning. Most are also well educated and hold responsible jobs.

But newbies are weak on strategy, word knowledge, and anagramming (forming words from random letters) skills. They are unaware of the countless hours of study that can make the moves of their seasoned opponents seem effortless. In short, they don't know that Scrabble is a learned skill. This can lead to embarrassment.

Take a recent night at the Denver club. A new player arrived late. I put my game on hold, said hello, gave her the "cheat sheet" (a list of two- and three-letter words), and paired her with another newcomer who had five or six sessions under his belt. About fifteen minutes later, when the woman got up, her head was down, and she was moving fast. I hoped their game had ended and she was dashing for the restroom, which is in the same direction as the door, but feared the worst. She bolted and was gone. I considered chasing her, but then what? Cajoling her in a dark, freezing alley didn't make much sense. Maybe she could have become a good player, but we'll never know.

For those who stick it out, timed games can be intimidating. Each player is allowed twenty-five minutes to complete his game. This means games are almost always over in fifty minutes or less. Players use a clock that has two dials. When a player finishes his turn he hits his opponent's clock which starts it running. Ten points are subtracted from a player's score for each minute that he goes over twenty-five. Games tend to move along. Many new players view this time constraint as daunting. It's not particularly demanding once one becomes accustomed to it, but it takes a while. Although it's only necessary to tally the total score each turn, what is mind-boggling to the newcomer is that a few advanced players will not only do that, but also write down the individual scores, the word that was played, the seven tiles of each rack, track the tiles that were played by both sides, and still not use all their time.

Perhaps the biggest difference for most new players is the constant losing. Most of those who give club play a whirl regularly trounce friends and relatives. In the process they have come to think of themselves as competent players. Still, most serious players, if asked how long they have played, will only count the time since their first club meeting; they feel that's when they began to "really" learn how to play. Yes, they knew the basic rules and how to place the tiles on the board, but when it came to strategy, word knowledge, and board awareness, they had little or none. Like virtually all newbies, they were thumped on their inaugural club visits, but they came back.

Most newcomers don't. In my ten years with the Denver club, over 100 players have tried us out and said no thanks. From what I've heard our rate of retention is not uncommon. Bernard Gotlieb, who has run the Montreal club since 1978, reports a similar experience. "I've seen in the neighborhood of 200 players come once and never come back," laments Gotlieb.

Some efforts are made to cushion the shock of club play. Free challenges, for one, whereby the newcomer can challenge the acceptability of a word, but not lose a turn if she's wrong. Most clubs also allow the use of a "cheat sheet." It contains all the two- and three-letter words, along with the four-letter J, Q, X, and Z words and "vowel dumps" like OORIE, LOUIE, and AWEE. The clock isn't strictly enforced, either. How long these crutches are permitted varies with the newcomer and the club.

Despite these concessions, clubs aren't able to retain more than a handful of players. Remember, these are the same people who initially called or e-mailed, enthused about playing their favorite game in a club setting. The responsibility for losing them falls on both the clubs and the new players. Club members often don't go out of their way to recruit these fresh faces, while organized Scrabble doesn't meet the expectations that many new players bring through the door.

Most neophytes, for example, believe Scrabble prowess is solely a function of intelligence and education. They vanquish their friends and family, and it must be because they are smart and got that M.A. in English. They don't realize that just like bridge, chess or calculus, tournament-style Scrabble is a learned skill. Native ability varies, but no one just walks in off the street and knows how to play. "The guy can be a brain surgeon with a huge vocabulary," says Gotlieb, "but if he doesn't know words like AA [a type of lava], he can't play. And why would he know a ridiculous word like that unless he was a geologist?" When most of these recruits come to realize the amount of effort they will have to expend to become competitive, they drop out.

It usually takes years to get some sort of handle on the game and a far from perfect one at that. Still, many new players expect to hold their own or even show club players a thing or two. Such a person is shocked and chagrinned by his first encounter with a real Scrabble player. Ginger White of Shirley, New York, who has run a club since 1982, puts it this way, "Newbies feel that they are being judged as people and in most cases their egos can't handle loss after loss."

There is something about matching wits over a Scrabble board that gets to the heart of who we are as literate people, or so it seems to the parlor player. It speaks to intelligence, education, all the things that we hold dear and by which many of us measure ourselves. To lose, especially to lose badly, and perhaps to someone who doesn't give the impression of erudition or brilliance, can be crushing and/or humiliating.

At the Denver club I've seen well-educated, intelligent newcomers struggle to maintain some semblance of their intellectual self-worth as they were pummeled senseless. I've played with people who say they have never lost, but within a turn or two demonstrate that they have no idea how to play. They quickly realize it too. Their cheeks turn red, they fidget and squirm and would like to be anywhere but where they are. One reason for that, says Albany's Goodman, is that Scrabble is marketed as a fun, family game. "Many people show up expecting games with three or four people at a table, conversation, potato chips, and soda." Instead, they find a serious, often cutthroat atmosphere.

Dennis Kaiser, who played in the Denver club, recalled that his first club experiences were "totally demoralizing." That was twenty years ago. He was an average parlor player then, but transformed himself into one of the top 100 in North America. When he started, though, he was terrible compared to the club regulars. "I would see how fast they would come up with plays," said Kaiser, "and I would just shake my head and think there is no way I am going to get my brain to work like that." After five or six sessions he wanted to quit, but Dan Unger, the club director, convinced him to stick it out. He did, and became a far better player than any of the people he once found so amazing.

Sometimes the attrition rate is not just a question of Scrabble skills. Sometimes it's plain rudeness. John Green, a relatively new player, attended the Los Gatos, California, club for the first time in 1997. His first game was with Stu Goldman, who came up in the New York City game rooms during the 1970s. After waxing Green by some 300 points, in a loud voice Goldman asked, "What's the club roadkill record?" A less competitive player might have called it quits, but not Green, who has since become an active club member and tournament organizer. Of course, he will never forget his first night at the Los Gatos club.

Losing and dealing with rudeness are only the tip of the

iceberg. Many new players don't want to devote time to the game. They consider it absurd when someone brings up studying. Many don't believe that it's possible to improve the speed of their play, their strategy, or their anagramming ability. Many think it's too much work. That is the way I saw it when I first played in the Honolulu Club in 1995. I joined at the group's inception, so the membership was one of modest abilities. Still I lost games. I realized I would have to study. So I dropped out after three sessions. Stormed out might be a better description of that last night. My wife continued, however, enjoyed considerable success, and had a good time too. After five or six weeks of listening to her war stories, I couldn't stand it any longer. I went back, got hooked, began a modest study program, and slowly became immersed in the game.

Because studying is hard work, people decide at various points along the way that they have had enough—that however good they are, that's good enough. Take Jim Miller, who has been playing in the San Diego club since 1992. Miller is rated in the 1700s (in the top 8% of players) and has put in his share of study time. Still, he recently commented that "I don't like having to constantly and dutifully keep cumbersome lists fresh in my memory." Miller is a word lover and that keeps him at the game. But he calls himself a "stagnant 1700s player" because right now he is not prepared to put in the time to go further.

There are other things besides studying that also turn off new players. Some are appalled by the way the game is played by more experienced club members. There's the clock, of course. Then there's the twenty-five page rulebook, compared to the box top or made-up rules they use at home. They can scare away the neophyte.

Another irritant for newbies is that most seasoned players don't concern themselves with word meanings. That throws many people because they consider themselves word lovers, and the game itself a test of vocabulary. The newcomer will see a word like AEOLIAN, ask what it means, and often get the response "You don't get any points for definitions, but we can look it up later." I recall the time that Brian Cappelletto appeared on the *Today Show* after winning the 1998 Nationals. Katie Couric asked him for a word without vowels. He gave her CWM (a steep-walled basin). She asked, "What does that mean?" He sheepishly responded, "I don't know."

There's also the matter of phony words. At home many people never use a word that isn't real. Not so at the clubs. In serious Scrabble it's "catch me if you can." If you do, I lose my turn. If you don't, too bad for you. This grates many newcomers the wrong way, since they associate bluffing with poker and other card games but not with a genteel game like Scrabble. When faced with so many new and what appear to be ridiculous looking words, phonies become even more of a problem.

Getting away with a phony is often abetted by the policy of giving new club members "free challenges"— that is, permitting them to challenge a word without losing a turn if they are wrong. A few veterans see this as an invitation to lay down any phony they want, but the newbie is often too embarrassed to take the free challenge and admit further ignorance, so the phony stays on the board. Later, if the phony comes to light, the new player feels cheated, while the old-timer can say "but he had free challenges."

Weird words are also a problem. There was a time,

twenty-five or thirty years ago, when Scrabble was essentially about being literate and well read. Most parlor players continue to view it this way. But once Scrabble is approached seriously, it becomes something else. Regardless of one's educational background, no one has a vocabulary that will go very far in organized Scrabble because most of the letterati memorize word lists. Typically this starts with the two- and three-letter words, then the fours, and so on. Words like KA, ORT, BHUT, and OURIE soon become second nature, but the newbie can only puzzle and shake his head.

That said, one might think that with new players such a scarce resource, that club members would fall all over themselves to welcome them into the fold. Not so. Certainly there are exceptions, but it has been my experience that club regulars tend to be caught up in their individual rivalries and don't go out of their way to make a newcomer feel appreciated. Milt Wertheimer recalled sessions in the early '90s at the strong Lauderhill club in Florida. Even though he was a seasoned player, he didn't have much fun. It was too serious, he said. As for the newcomers, "The club players weren't friendly, everyone was cliquish and kept to themselves. Who in the hell would want to go back?"

Kathryn Northcut, who used to play in the Fort Collins, Colorado, club has a theory about that. She thinks that Scrabble tends to attract the introvert. So a new player may get a modest welcome and then go an entire evening without exchanging more than a sentence or two. Northcut says she was terrified to go to her first club session because she's not a joiner and doesn't like meeting people. "But I was by far the most outspoken and gregarious member of our group." Les Schonbrun, who came up in the New York game clubs in the 1960s, has made similar observations. "I found games a way to be with people," says Schonbrun, "and keep my distance at the same time. The board is between you. You don't have to deal with the messy questions of do I want to hang around with this person or not, things that are hard for the shy and insecure, like me, and like so many others." Are there outgoing people in organized Scrabble? Sure. But it's probably safe to say that most of those who move toward the top of the ratings are not exactly party animals.

At least one group has tried to ease the passage from parlor to club play. For almost ten years Susi Tiekert (and now Joel Sherman) ran a newcomer's group for the high-powered Club No. 56 in New York. It met twice a month for two hours. During these sessions Tiekert tried to impart the basics of tournament level Scrabble. Newbies were taught the rules, jargon, and protocols of the game. They also got to play Tiekert, a tournament veteran. To graduate they had to know all the acceptable two-letter words—about ninety. Tiekert also made sure that they were indoctrinated "in the silence and seriousness of the game" so that they didn't disrupt the club with unnecessary socializing. She told them to be prepared to lose their first fifty games to club regulars.

If the New York approach could be called coddling, and many would, there appears to be very little of it in North American clubs. We recruit the people who can take a licking and keep on ticking. For some club members it is sort of a macho thing: "We want a few good people." That typical, first night experience, though, goes something like this: the newcomer gets beaten badly, probably humiliated, does not have fun, and does not make friends. This means he has to be very competitive and truly want to learn the game to return. At least that's the conclusion of club director Ginger White. "Only the competitive, thick-skinned player will not give up," says White.

Very few players question this approach. It's always been done this way. Those of us who soldiered on were so busy trying to learn, compete and fit in, we didn't pay much attention to the vast majority who fell by the wayside. We were proud that we survived. They, on the other hand, didn't have the right stuff. Periodically, we scratch our heads, lament the small size of our club, and ask why there aren't more than ten or twelve people in the Denver metropolitan area who want to play organized Scrabble. Perhaps it shouldn't be such a mystery.

10

As Good As One's Word

Learning the Lexicon

In 1991 Bob Lipton, of Vero Beach, Florida, was having dinner with Charlie Southwell and some other players during a break in the Cincinnati Masters Tournament. Somewhere between the appetizers and the desserts Southwell looked at the menu, cocked his head, and said, "I'll pick up the check for anyone who can tell me all the eight letter words you can make with POLENTA and a blank." Lipton promptly rattled off PANTOFLE, CONEPATL, GANTLOPE, ANTELOPE, ANTIPOLE, PENTANOL, and POLENTAS. Bon appetit, Bob. But more importantly, how did he do that?

Learning the words is no simple matter. If it were, the world would be awash in great Scrabble players. It's not always easy to get people to talk about how they acquired their word knowledge, or to know if you are getting a straight answer when they do. A player might say he seldom studies to give his opponents a false sense of security or inferiority. He might exaggerate the time he puts in to intimidate the opposition. Or since studying is a solitary, time-consuming activity, he might want to keep his reclusive tendencies to himself.

No one ever learns all the words, of course, but most of the best players are always trying. It's easy to see why. In most board games, chess and checkers for example, the game pieces are fixed in number and often in place when the contest begins. Not so in Scrabble where the words, slightly more than 100,000 of them, are considered the game pieces, not the tiles. They reside in the players' heads. Learning them, though, is like washing the windows of a skyscraper: by the time the job is done, it's time to start again. Some words are forgotten, others confused, and now and again words are added to, or dropped from, the *Official Club and Tournament Word List* (OWL).

Learning a lot of words is one of the things that separates the parlor from the tournament player. With a few exceptions, the higher a player is ranked the more words she will know. Of course, knowing more words than your opponent doesn't guarantee victory. There's strategy, luck of the draw, and the ability to extract the words in your head from the tiles on your rack, among other things. A quick example. Most of us would take one look at the highly improbable rack of AGIOUUY and groan. But a top player would see OUGUIYA, a monetary unit of Mauritania.

The letterati take pride in their word knowledge. After a match it's not uncommon for a kibbitzer to ask, "Why didn't you play OCARINA in turn four?" Players also get more satisfaction from slapping down a word like RETIARII than RETAINS, even if they score the same number of points, because this demonstrates prowess. It's not unheard of for someone to play an unusual word when a more prosaic alternative is the strategically best play, because the unusual word is proof of a long-term study commitment. And then there's the challenged word. To draw a challenge from a better player and win, now that's the best.

The parlor player knows little or nothing about these things. He thinks he is good because he is well read and has a Ph.D. That's all the ammunition he needs. The tournament player knows otherwise. Joel Wapnick, for example, has an Ed.D., teaches at McGill University in Montreal, and has won the North American, Canadian, and World championships. Although Wapnick began his study regimen in 1976, he still tries to get in his two hours a day.

There is no right way to do it. Personal preferences are important. One method may be more efficient than another, but that makes little difference if a player won't use it. Robert Felt recommended trying to make it fun. But for most, it's work—whether it's reading the *Official Scrabble Players Dictionary*, memorizing flash cards, or sitting down with a computer study program.

Les Schonbrun began pushing tiles in the 1960s and learned the game in the New York chess clubs playing low-stakes money games. Schonbrun says he actively dislikes studying. He didn't study in the 1960s and says, "If my opponents were studying they didn't talk about it." On his way to the top he played people who were more skilled and learned from them. To improve his word knowledge he did crossword puzzles and read a lot. The need to study was brought home to him in the 1980

Nationals when upstart Joe Edley—a player he once beat handily—won the tournament, and Schonbrun finished well back in the pack. Joe had been studying. He was "booked up," says Schonbrun. Today Schonbrun still resists studying. "Definitely no schedule or discipline about it," he says. But thirty-five years of experience holds him in good stead.

Stu Goldman got his Scrabble legs at Chess City, a New York City club. In the mid 1970s Goldman decided to try a tournament. In preparation he bought a *Funk & Wagnalls College Dictionary*, then culled out the two-letter words. That was his introduction to studying. He remembers vividly his first anagramming breakthrough. As he worked with the word COUPONS he realized that the same letters spelled SOUPCON. "I got a tremendous rush, and that was the beginning of a marked improvement in my anagramming ability," says Goldman.

By the time of the first Nationals in 1978 Goldman was already considered a good player. He wrote "Bag to Board," a column for *Scrabble Players Newspaper* and ran the Long Island club. His approach to studying had also become more ambitious. He knew the importance of the seven- and eight-letter words—their fifty extra bonus points. To bone up for the Nationals he took several thousand address labels, printed a word on one side and its jumbled letters on the other—a flashcard of sorts. He would draw the labels out of a paper bag and unscramble the letters on the commuter train into New York.

Another person who learned a lot of words while on the go is Jerry Lerman. He lives outside of San Francisco, but rides the bus in every day. Lerman began serious play with the publication of the *Official Scrabble Players*

Dictionary in 1978. He and Joe Edley would spar each week at the Meat Market Coffeehouse in Noe Valley, San Francisco. When Edley won the Nationals in 1980, says Lerman, "I knew I must be getting pretty good because I was beating him twenty percent of the time."

Lerman was never the type to allow his world to revolve around Scrabble. With a family and a full-time job, he says, "I had to fit studying into the nooks and crannies of my life." So he would always carry the *Official Scrabble Players Dictionary* on his bus ride to work. He didn't have a real plan, but would just skip around. "If I remembered the word NEMATODE from biology, I might start there," says Lerman, "to see what words began with NEM-, which might lead to NEPENTHE and so on."

And then there's Bob Lipton, who rattled off all the POLENTA words to win the dinner from Charlie Southwell. Lipton uses anamonics to keep track of large numbers of words. In simplest terms, an anamonic is a phrase that helps the player remember a group of words made up of similar letters, like the seven-letter word POLENTA plus a blank. Although Lipton was among the first to develop and use anamonics in the late 1980s, Nick Ballard, a retired San Francisco player, receives much of the credit for them because of his 1992 compendium *Anamonics #1–2100*, to which many expert players contributed.

The most rewarding anamonic is the one that goes with the stem TISANE. Tisane is a tea. The anamonic phrase is "Makes Excellent Herb Tea Giving Food A Powerful Buzz." Each unique letter in the phrase (there are twenty-three) when combined with TISANE will make at least one seven-letter word; there are sixty-nine words from ACETINS to ZANIEST. The letterati who use anamonics learn hundreds or even thousands, though some expert players think anamonics are more trouble than they are worth. Not Lipton—he has developed his own hybrid system that encompasses thousands of six-letter stems.

Lipton also took an unusual approach to committing his words and anamonics to memory. Prior to retirement, he worked as a croupier on the graveyard shift (4 a.m. to 12 noon) at the Horseshoe Hotel and Casino in Las Vegas. "Some, but not all the time," says Lipton, "business was dead or dying at the beginning of the shift." Over a two and a half year period, he spent roughly two hours a night working Scrabble racks in his head rather than daydreaming his shift away.

Brian Cappelletto, arguably North America's top player, says he's "old school" when it comes to learning words. Back in the mid 1980s, when he was fifteen or so, he got Mike Baron's *Bingo Book* and made flashcards for all the seven- and eight-letter words that he didn't know. He feels there is a lot to be learned from the process, things that the person who uses computer-generated lists doesn't know he is missing. "It's the difference between learning your way around a city," says Cappelletto, "and memorizing a map."

The letterati have also come up with some oddball ways to learn words. Take Travis Chaney. When he worked the night shift cleaning floors at a Wal-Mart in Arkansas, he found a way to make his work time into study time. "I often attached word lists to the buffing machine," he says, "so that I could study while I cleaned."

Pat Barrett, one of the top women players in the country, credits some of her success to listening to word tapes. In twenty years she has amassed some sixty hours worth, which she often listens to while driving. Steve Dennis, who plays in the Atlanta club, studies electronically. Once a month he makes the 700-mile drive to Cincinnati, but he doesn't make it alone. Buckled into the passenger seat is his laptop computer, which is running LeXpert, a word study program. "Every eight seconds I glance at the screen, note the letters, and then look back at the road while I try to unscramble them in my head."

Traveling in place is another option. Some fifteen years ago Steve Glass, who plays out of the Dallas, Texas, club, came up with a neat way to learn all the words with RE-, OUT-, UN-, OVER-, DE-, SUB-, and BE- prefixes. "I memorized them daily for two years while doing stair-stepping machine workouts," says Glass.

Carol Shaver, who played at the Gainesville, Florida, club, took up Scrabble at age sixty-five, and felt that she needed some kind of gimmick to keep all her new-found words straight. Shaver came up with bawdy bingo narratives for the first fifty bingo stems, like TISANE. "They are not suitable for publicaton," says Shaver, "but the main thing was to use what was familiar or unforgettable." Shaver needed to do more than see the words, so she arranged, recited, sang, and rhymed them. Here's her SATIRE stem plus a T: The ARTIEST ARTISTE is IRATEST when eating TASTIER RATITES in STRIATE ATTIRES.

Though all this work is necessary, it doesn't make the "booked up" player infallible. Everyone commits miscues. My memory at sixty-four, for example, is not what it once was. I've challenged good words, only to realize later, that I once knew and had played them. I struggle to keep some words straight—take CALIX, CALYX, CYLIX, and KYLIX, and still confuse them in the heat of competition.

Yet, study one must. I've used audio tapes, paper lists, LeXpert (a word study program), and flashcards too. In periods of high enthusiasm I've spent hours each day, week in and out, staring at racks as they unfolded across my computer screen. I've fought eye strain and droopy lids with coffee, showers, and walks around the house.

Is it worth it? There's a joy to Scrabble that makes it both addictive and satisfying. Whatever the outcome on a given day, players invariably return. An elusive eight-letter word is found for the first time. A strategic concept that never made sense becomes crystal clear. Defensive tactics that were once a chore to recall, become automatic. Tiles that would have looked hopeless a year ago, offer scoring possibilities. The game comes together, piece by piece. This is why players do it.

11

The Seven Tile Obsession

Going to Extremes

There's no need to quibble about the clinical ins and outs of obsession. Let's just say that Scrabble tends to take over the lives of those who play it at the club and tournament level. They exhibit behavior that most of the rest of the world would consider a bit odd. In fact, many of the letterati are a little wacky when it comes to Scrabble. At least one has taken it with him into therapy, which he thinks has improved his game.

There's something about Scrabble that is irresistable for those who play it seriously. It's not uncommon, for example, to hear dedicated players say they need their Scrabble fix. Even if a recent club or tournament outing was a disaster, within a day or two, most can't wait to compete again. And it's not all joy. Anyone who has walked the length of a tournament room and examined the faces of the participants can testify to that. The game can make you miserable, but quitting isn't really an option. Not many people hang up their racks.

This Scrabble obsession can lead to some pretty bizarre behavior. The letterati see a new word in the newspaper or hear it on TV and are compelled to look it up. Could it be good? They know TRUNDLER and TRINDLE, and one day it hits them, what about TRINDLER? They look it up. Scrabble players daydream about words on the job, and struggle with racks while they sleep. They review word lists as they doze off and even get up to check on spellings when confused.

The mania extends to everyday conversation too. Jerry Lerman, an expert California player and Wells Fargo executive, recalls the time that he killed a conversation about company policy when he blurted out that POLICY plus ET forms EPICOTYL and LIPOCYTE. "Although they didn't ostracize me," says Lerman, "it made me feel like a schnook to have broken up the conversation with such meaningless drivel."

Family and friends learn that it's not such a good idea to ask, "How's Scrabble going?" In response, a serious player might launch into tales of his latest study regimen or tournament gaffe. Serious Scrabble is an acquired taste. The further into the game a player goes, the more removed he becomes from the parlor player's understanding of Scrabble. Only fellow loonies get it.

It begins with playing. Before joining the Honolulu club in 1995, my wife and I would play once a week with friends. When a couple at the club said that they played every night after supper, we just rolled our eyes. Not anymore. I'll play the computer a couple of games to wake up in the morning and probably a couple during the day. If I wake up at night, I'll play 'til I get drowsy.

Everyone plays too much, in the sense that the time could be better spent studying. Les Schonbrun sometimes does little else but play the computer for days on end. There's an allure and irresistible challenge to playing a machine. An adversarial relationship develops between player and program. The computer beats most players most of the time (but today will be different).

A few years back Dan Brinkley, a relative newcomer to Scrabble, inquired of his fellow online addicts if he was odd because he carried word lists in his wallet and often an electronic Scrabble dictionary, known as a Franklin, with him at all times. His friends thought he was "ill and in need of medical help."

"Relax. You're normal," responded Zev Kaufman, an expert Canadian player. "I've been addicted for fifteen years. I take my Franklin with me everywhere." The same went for Bill Palmer, a former Boulder, Colorado, player, who always carried three Franklins. That way he could have different lists running at the same time. According to New York's David Stone, "I've worn out three Franklins. I always have one with me." Lynne Butler added, "I have word lists on the wall in the kitchen, by the phone, in the bathroom, and in my car." Butler also has Maven, the Scrabble playing program, on the school computer where she works, so she can play at lunch.

The company that made the Franklin electronic dictionary ceased production in the mid '90s. That, combined with its flimsy keyboard, meant that not many people owned working models after 2000 or so. I bought a half dozen in a 1998 closeout sale for $35 each and kept one in all the places I studied. I kept one in my Scrabble bag, too. Times changed: all but one of my Franklins are kaput, several thousand words have been added to the lexicon, and I've upgraded to a PDA, as have most players.

This insatiable desire for words goes hand-in-hand with Scrabble addiction. At the 1998 National Championship, some of the participants went over to the Art Institute of Chicago one night. At one point seven or eight players were gathered around a particular painting, but rather than looking at it, they were thumbing their Franklins. The word FOULARD was in the painting's title and they wanted to know if it was good. It is. Not to be outdone, one player explored the medieval armor display, jotting a list of old English words as she went.

Yet words are just the half of it. Diane Firstman, of New York, went to the hospital to see her mother through gall bladder surgery. When Firstman arrived her mother was already under the knife. She called Roz Gold, another New York player, for a bit of commiseration. One thing led to another, Gold went to the hospital, just happened to have her Scrabble gear, and soon they were playing in Diane's mother's room. The game was in progress when her mother was wheeled in. "I was the slightest bit disappointed we didn't get to finish," Firstman says.

Glenda Short and Lee Brooks, of Oklahoma City, drive to tournaments all around the country and break the travel tedium at roadside parks where they stop to play. "We are deterred only by high winds, downpours, and fire ants," says Short.

After competing in the Western Championship, Lester Schonbrun and Mitch Bayersdorfer were on their way home and had five hours to kill at the Reno airport. Scrabble seemed to be the obvious thing to do, but they had checked their boards. Mitch did have a bag of tiles, though. They drew the center star of the Scrabble game board on a McDonald's tabletop and off they went.

In 1984 and '85 Stu Goldman took a sabbatical from his New York teaching job to visit museums and schools throughout the United States and Canada. He stayed with Scrabble players along the way, and played in dozens of cities, clubs, and homes. What did he call it? "That's easy," he says, "a Scrabbatical."

As you can imagine, such people wouldn't let many things stand in the way of getting to their weekly club meetings. The Gulf War was just an inconvenience for the Jerusalem club, according to Sam Orbaum. Over a six-week period, while Americans were glued to their TVs watching for incoming Scuds, some three dozen Israelis were glued to their chairs watching for incoming bingos. Speaking through gas masks added a new dimension to announcing scores and making challenges.

If you were to think about activities in which participants "play hurt," Scrabble would probably never cross your mind. Think again. Although they lack trainers, whirlpools, and team physicians, and seldom compete for more than a pittance in prize money, tournament tile pushers often mix it up under some very dicey conditions. It's not a question of suffering bodily injury over the board, but rather that the letterati bring their maladies with them and play through the pain.

Mike Willis, of Dallas, is of the opinion that physical adversity improves his concentration. One time Willis' radiator cap blew, filled his shirt with a mixture of scalding water and antifreeze, and peeled the skin off his torso. Five hours in the emergency room and five morphine shots later he emerged swathed in bandages. The next night he got rewrapped and headed straight for his club. "I showed a few people the bandages," says Willis, "to prove what a true Scrabble player will endure to play."

In 1997, Charlene Bishop, a Seattle player, was rushed to the hospital for emergency gall-bladder surgery. There were complications, and some thought Charlene had played her last seven-letter word. When she got out of intensive care, Eileen Gruhn went visiting with her Scrabble gear, just in case. She found Bishop hooked up to all manner of tubes and drips, with a temperature of 105. But, says Gruhn, when Bishop saw the board, her eyes lit up. Bishop 385, Gruhn 340, nursing staff bewildered.

Steve Pellinen didn't fare as well. He and Lisa Odom, both top Minnesota players, were on their way to Dallas, Texas, for the 1996 Nationals. They had overnighted in Fayetteville, Arkansas, and were packing their car when the improbable happened. Pellinen had just bent down to empty some trash under the motel's second floor steps when he felt a whack to the head that dropped him in his tracks. He'd stood up too quickly and dinged his forehead on the underside of the stairs. There was a two-inch gash and blood everywhere. He got stitched up, and off they went. When they reached Dallas, Pellinin's lethargy and dizziness lifted and he decided to play. His wound was bruised and oozing blood and pus. He figured, "If it made my opponents half as nauseous as it made me I thought I'd stand a chance." His opponents expressed shock and concern and then proceeded to thrash him without apology.

Some players cope with chronic medical problems. Willie Swank-Pitzer of Dayton, Ohio, has had MS for twenty-five years and continues to play tournaments.

Sometimes she plays in a baseball cap and dark glasses to shut out glare and other visual stimuli. Sitting can be a problem too, which is just what tournament play requires, sometimes up to eight hours a day. She takes along heating pads and plenty of liniment. Recently she experienced temporary blindness. "I got scared about going totally blind and not being able to go to tournaments," she says, "so I went to eleven last year."

Frank Lee, a Cincinnati player, says, "There's nothing very sexy about playing sick." Lee has post-polio syndrome and can be recognized by his gray beard, stovepipe hat, and wheelchair. "You're actually playing two opponents," says Lee. "There's the person sitting across the table and the person taking jabs at your ribcage, spine, shoulders, hips, and head."

Sam Orbaum, of Israel, tells the "best last word" story. Harold Bloom attended the Jerusalem club on December 20, 1988. Harold was an original member, a wonderful guy, beloved by everyone, said Orbaum. Harold, who was seventy-five, was matched up with Ami Tzubery, a young Yemenite Israeli. "He played GANGLION," said Orbaum, "lurched forward, and died." No doubt the way many of the letterati would like to go.

Attending tournaments or even playing in clubs is not what most people would call relaxing. Players compete in tournaments for anywhere from five to eight hours a day for at least two days and possibly as many as five. They become fatigued, on edge. Faces are grim, some frustrated, others devastated. Everyone feels the strain. Sometimes players engage in boorish behavior.

Boorish might be a stretch to describe what happened

to Janet Rice, but if nothing else it was rude. In 1999 Rice combined a family visit with entering her first tournament, which was held in the Pocono Mountains. She hadn't studied or used a clock. Opponents got exasperated with her playing, her scoring, and her all-round inexperience. One man didn't want to play her. A woman told her she should have stayed home. Rice ended up in tears. These boorish behaviors can even happen to seasoned players. Take Shirley Fliesser, who is rated over 1600, and who beat a well-known top player, although she declines to name him. "He called me a bag of shit and stalked off," she says, although he later apologized.

Another top woman who recently had a problem is Jan Dixon. She has played tournament Scrabble since the early 1980s and has at various times been the top female player in the country. Even so, in early 2000 she got bushwacked by another expert player. Dixon's last game had run long, then she discovered she was out of her custom score sheets. She made a dash for her room to get more. When she returned she found her clock had been started, her opponent had made his first play, and she'd already been docked five minutes. The tournament director sided with her opponent. She was late. Too bad. Dixon was livid, but to make matters worse, as she readied herself, and with her clock ticking, she had to listen to her opponent taunting her with "come on, come on, make your play." She feels her lack of time and frayed emotions contributed to her loss. Because she couldn't shake off the incident, she even took several months off from the game. Although her position was later vindicated (her clock should not have been started), she says she has never received an apology from her opponent.

On rare occasions boorish players get their comeup-

Charlie Southwell congratulates Jan Dixon after she won the first C Note tournament in 1984. Mike Martin, the Game Room's "Head Prazy," looks on.

pance. Some players are always complaining. The tiles are terrible, the opponent is so lucky, the board is just right—for you, and so on. One such person, according to Sam Orbaum, was paired in a tournament with fifteen-year-old Ben Bloom of Tel Aviv. He played despite his cerebral palsy, which made him contort and shake uncontrollably. The woman he played had complained throughout their game, which she eventually lost. At the end she said, "I can't believe your luck." Bloom leaned right into her face, his legs shaking, his mouth contorted and loudly said, "Lady, you call this lucky?" The place went nuts, said Orbaum, and the woman was never seen again.

Two longtime players who compete near the top are known for their tournament outbursts. In 2000 they both showed up for a tournament in Daytona, Florida. Before it was over a number of complaints were filed with the NSA. The primary problem was noise in the form of obscenities hurled at the tiles, the game, and some players. There apparently was a rack-throwing incident too, along with disparaging comments on the play of various participants. One of the troublemakers, Marlon Hill, unapologetically says, "I was horrible in Florida, although I don't recall throwing around anything but four-letter words."

What made it worse, says Barbara Horsting, a Florida player, is that when asked to be quiet, one of the players became belligerent. The other also made racist comments and when told that he would be cited for this behavior, threatened future violence, according to a witness who would prefer to remain anonymous. One of the boors, Gordon Shapiro, who was in many ways a likeable rogue, said he almost got thrown out of the NSA because of the incident. "I threatened one of the players," said the long-time Maryland tile pusher.

There were so many complaints to the NSA, with some people wondering if they had legal recourse, that the NSA Advisory Board met to discuss the problem. Out of that came a new rule that gives directors the right to eject players for what "is deemed to be inappropriate and/or unsportsmanlike behavior." John Williams, NSA's Executive Director, also emphasized that the NSA was prepared to suspend players from tournament competition for serious infractions.

But even that wasn't enough. At the 2002 Nationals in San Diego, Williams announced another escalation of policy regarding crude behavior. Apparently, there had been further incidents of intimidation at both clubs and tournaments. It would not be tolerated. "One incident and you are out," said Williams. No more club or tournament play.

Scrabble events are far from a Wild West show. Most of the letterati, most of the time, are well behaved. As with any group, though, Scrabble has its bad boys. Combine them with the intense, competitive ambience of club and tournament play and there can be fireworks. It helps to be thick skinned or to develop one, because Scrabble is a full contact mind sport.

12

Ethics

Playing Fast and Loose

To the parlor player the role of ethics in Scrabble probably seems a stretch. You just lay down the tiles and count the points, right? How complicated can that be? Very, if you are a gamesman. Club and tournament players are always trying to get a leg up.

When a player lackadaisically puts down SLOANINE through an L, instead of SOLANINE, as I did a few nights ago, does his opponent say, "Hey, you need to reverse the O and L"? Of course not. The opponent gleefully challenges and blocks the spot. Or when Player A fails to start Player B's clock, which gives B free thinking time, does B say anything? Not likely.

Once new club players get over the odd words, the solemnity of the occasion, and the strength of their new-found playing partners, there is still one more hurdle to overcome—the phony. Perhaps the playing of phony words is the biggest shocker to parlor players. Many view it as underhanded, but it's an integral part of organized play. There are rules of thumb about when to play phonies and actual lists of promising candidates—non-words that are very seductive in their word-like qualities, such as ARSEHOLE and BURPERS. Some tournaments offer a small prize for the most creative phony. Although not everyone approves of phonies, everyone uses them now and then.

The pros and cons of the phony have been with us from the start. The October 1981 *Scrabble Players Newspaper* was largely devoted to the matter. There were articles on how to bluff and how to challenge. One article asked why we allow phonies in a word game that is supposed to test vocabulary. Wasn't that counter to the spirit of the game? It comes down to this: nothing in the rules prevents phonies. What's more, even someone who claims he never plays an intentional phony still puts down a misspelled or misremembered word now and then. Conclusion: the best defense against a phony is to learn as many words as possible.

In North America the double challenge rule is used. This means that if a word is challenged the challenger loses her turn if the word is correct, while the player of the word loses her turn if the word is a phony. This contrasts with the single challenge rule used in the United Kingdom. There, the challenger does not lose a turn if the word is good. This leads to more challenges, the playing of fewer phony words, and the loss of the bluffing element of the game. At the same time, some would argue that it makes for a more harmonious/civilized atmosphere because even though one person is outplayed he isn't outslicked.

North American player Bob Felt, argued the double

challenge rule is superior to the British approach because it rewards bravery, requires fine judgment and nerves and encourages players to try words they aren't sure of. It also encourages players to study their opponent's style of play. What is their word knowledge? Under what circumstances do they challenge? "These kinds of psychological skills," argued Felt, "are significantly eroded by free challenges." What about holding back a potential phony? Felt considered it equivalent to self-flagellation. As gamesmen are fond of saying, when a potential phony hits the board, four things can happen and three of them are good: the word isn't challenged and it's bad; it isn't challenged and it's good (it happens); it's challenged and it's good; it's challenged and it's bad. That sounds like pretty good odds to many Scrabble players.

This approach raises some interesting questions. Luise Shafritz, an expert player who lives in Las Vegas, Nevada, doesn't like bluffing. She says it "cheapens the game and puts it on a level with poker." Veteran players can take advantage of less-experienced players, since the newer players are well aware that their opponents have larger vocabularies. The superior player realizes that too and can exploit the situation. Sometimes, it becomes the way the more-experienced player neutralizes the luck of the draw. Still, there are others who are not so quick to take vows of abstinence and will lay down a phony whenever they think they can.

Shafritz, who is not alone in this, is particularly concerned about the effect of phonies on new club members. "Most new players just walk away in disgust," she says, which she contends reduces the ranks of the organized game. She asks, "What kind of feeling do you get when you realize you've lost a game because you didn't challenge a word?" According to Shafritz, Scrabble should be about word knowledge and strategy not bluffing.

Canadian Adam Logan feels that phonies are another facet of word knowledge and strategy. "I make it a practice to play words I'm not sure of often enough that some phonies go on the board. If nothing else, it makes it more likely that my good words will be challenged." Les Schonbrun, a top California player, says, "It stings to lose and it stings worse to be outplayed or outsmarted, no matter how. I don't see why phonies are better or worse than any other way of outsmarting someone."

Jim Geary, an expert player from Phoenix, recalls the time in 1995 when he played Mark Nyman, a UK player, in the Super Stars competition in Las Vegas. The dictionary was the North American OSPD. At one point Geary played HEROISE against the 1993 World Champion. He knew it was good in the UK with either an S or a Z, but that in North America only HEROIZE was acceptable. He suspected Nyman wouldn't know this. Forty points for Geary. He didn't feel guilty, either. "I felt bad," says Geary, "that I had to take the D hook, denying myself the chance to screw him out of a turn as well," by which he meant that he would have challenged HEROISES or HEROISED if Nyman had used the hook.

In Calgary, Alberta, Albert Hahn went up against Wayne Clifford, a fellow club member. Clifford had opened with WUD (which means insane), while Hahn had VAKEELS (which means an Indian lawyer) on his rack and wanted badly to play it. He couldn't make a parallel move and knew WUD didn't take an S. Hahn decided a phony was in order; Clifford would probably challenge it off the board, then play, and create a hook for VAKEELS. Hahn played KLEVA, with the A under the W in WUD, which formed WA, just as phony as KLEVA. Clifford had the right to challenge until Hahn withdrew a tile from the bag. Hahn tells the story: "I'm slowly reaching for the tile bag. I'm slowly sticking my hand in. I'm slowly rattling around in the bag giving him every opportunity to challenge but the son-of-a-gun is totally oblivious to either phony." Goodbye, VAKEELS.

Then there are times when the phony is good. This happened to Johnny Nevarez, an expert California player, who laid down what he thought was a phony, in the hope of getting it challenged. As Les Schonbrun remembers it, the word was challenged, but found acceptable. Not to be denied, according to Schonbrun, Nevarez did the unheard of thing of asking the word judge for a second opinion to invalidate his own word, which he lost. Possibly the only time a challenging player has attempted to prove his own play was no good.

Whatever one's feelings about phonies, the rubber meets the road when an opponent says "hold," which means he's considering a challenge. At that point, no one who is uncertain of his play wants it questioned. Theoretical considerations aside, he wants the points. He wants the win. He wants to slip one by. So he tries to look confident, indifferent, and hopes his opponent will lose his nerve. That's the way it is.

Playing phonies, though, is not the only ethical dilemma that competitors face. Take what's called coffeehousing. It's a tactic from New York City in the '60s and '70s when a lot of Scrabble was played in coffee houses. To coffeehouse is to distract or mislead. You can talk, rustle papers, cough, or anything else that breaks your opponent's concentration. Or you can use misdirection. Comments like "Oh God," or grimaces, or groans after drawing tiles. Are they spontaneous expressions of frustration, or calculated ploys to deceive your opponent? The matter has given rise to the advice: "Never pay any attention to what your opponent says."

Another way to coffeehouse is to intentionally mispronounce a word in the hope of drawing a challenge. For example pronouncing RESTING as RE-STING. Then there is wordless coffeehousing, also designed to provoke a challenge. Stu Goldman, of San Francisco, recalls the advice given in the old days about how to play the word TARZAN, a word many people would be unfamilar with and likely to challenge. "It should be played very quickly," says Goldman, "and then with an aghast slap on one's cheek, as if to say, 'What have I done?'"

All of these behaviors are considered pushing the envelope a bit, yet it's not always easy to draw the line or complain. It's hard to say that someone who drums the table, coughs a lot, or continually drops his pen is coffeehousing or just nervous. So does the offended party risk a scene by calling the person to task? A complaint will probably prove fruitless anyway, and perhaps frazzle the offended party's nerves to boot. Complain or move on?

Somewhat related to coffeehousing are pre-game comments intended to throw the other player off his stride or to get him to let his guard down. Adam Logan, one of the game's best, gets irked by people who say things like "It's such an honor to play you." He feels it's possible some people are sincere, "but I just try to ignore it," since he knows they are about to go after him tooth-and-nail and should they win, will tell their friends about it for months.

Some players are annoyed by what they call "bingo dumping." The "dumper" has a seven-letter word. He doesn't place the tiles on the board one at a time; he slides them off his rack so the letters fall into place like an alphabetical Slinky. There's no rule against it, but it still rubs many people the wrong way. Players view it as "in your face behavior," says Scott Pianowski, of the Lexington, Massachusetts, club.

Pianowski says "bingo dumping" is a "lame ritual," a way to say, "Hey, look at me." Some people who do it, like John Babina, John Attamack, or Pat Cole, claim it's just a time-saving device and they aren't changing. Adds Cole, "What's the harm in a little celebration now and then?"

Even counting the score has its pitfalls. Some people are not very good at it; they seem to be math impaired. Players who can count tend to get annoyed. This bad math raises an interesting question. If you see your opponent make a mathematical error, are you morally obligated to point it out even though the rules don't demand it? Or, since Scrabble is a mental game in which mental errors often cause one party to lose, is a scoring mistake just another mental error?

At the 1998 Nationals in Chicago, Zev Kaufman, a Canadian player, went over his score sheets after the tournament and discovered he had given an opponent an extra sixty points. Even though Kaufman was announcing the cumulative score after each turn, his opponent said nothing when Kaufman misread a two as an eight, did his addition, and announced 358 instead of 298. To Kaufman's surprise, when he brought the error to the attention of his opponent, who also went over his score sheets, the opponent claimed that he had also made a sixty-point error and on the same play, which allowed their score sheets to jibe. Kaufman complained to the NSA, but was told that it was not against the rules to make a scoring error, and that he didn't have conclusive proof of skullduggery. Kaufman won the game, but because of the scoring error finished ninth instead of eighth. The players no longer speak.

Some people, at least some of the time, purposely underscore themselves. The ploy is called "point banking." It will only work if the other player is not mentally recounting each play or is happy to let his opponent short change himself. The tactic can work in two ways. In a close game the plays made near the end may well change depending on whether a player thinks he is winning or losing by one score rather than another. If only the point banker knows the true score, then she is at an advantage, even if the underscoring never comes to light. But suppose the square shooter goes on to win by ten points, while the point banker knows he has an extra twelve points in the bank? He can then confidently ask for a recount, knowing that he will pull out a victory. Is this a common practice? Probably not, but it has a name and players talk about it.

Over the years various rules have been introduced to curb questionable practices. Each time an ambiguity crops up or some new method of cheating is uncovered, players lobby to close the loophole. This has gotten to the point that some players feel that with a twenty-five-page rulebook, things have gone too far, while others think every conceivable situation should be addressed. Take announcing the cumulative score.

Traditionally most people have announced after hitting their clock—in other words, on their opponent's time. A new rule says it must be announced on your time. The reasoning is that if it's done on your time, if it happens to break your opponent's concentration, at least he isn't losing valuable thinking time off his clock.

At a recent Las Vegas tournament, Mark Milan, of California, decided he would enforce the rule against Stu Goldman, who had a twenty-five-year habit of announcing his score after hitting his clock and had annoyed Milan in the past. Milan warned Goldman of his intentions before the game. When Goldman announced on Milan's time anyway, Milan warned him again. The next time it happened he called the tournament director, Paul Terry, who could have assessed a fifty-point penalty, but decided the infraction was not intentional and refused to cite Goldman. "Terry told me I was being picky," says a still-ticked Milan. Did Goldman intend to coffeehouse Milan? Did Milan mean to coffeehouse Goldman? Were both parties victims of circumstance? Goldman still feels put upon, while Milan feels wronged.

In the early 1980s, players used sand timers, moves could take no more than three minutes, a warning was issued six minutes before the game ended, and after sixty minutes the game was over even if all the tiles had not been played. Tiles left on a player's rack were deducted from the total score or added to the score of an opponent who had played all her tiles. In a close game, Susi Tiekert was playing Marlene Krell. Tiekert says, "[Krell] timed her last move to coincide with the end of the game, leaving me with a full rack to be subtracted from my score, and I lost. I've resented her ever since."

Some find the "fast bag artist" equally egregious. After a play is made the turn actually ends once the clock is hit, the score is tabulated, and at least one tile is drawn from the bag by the person who has just played. Sometimes, when an intentional phony is laid down or a player realizes she has accidentally put one down (say transposing two letters), she'll make a quick draw from the bag in the hope of officially ending the turn, before her opponent can spot the phony and enter a challenge.

For most people, cheating at Scrabble isn't worth the embarrassment and humiliation that would come with getting caught. There is very little money at stake, no national recognition, no endorsement deals, and other perks are nonexistent. No one knows how much cheating occurs, but there are rumors. This is a murky area because individual matches are monitored by the participants. This gives the cheater an edge.

For the most part, though, cheating is something that isn't talked about. The letterati prefer to think that organized Scrabble is more like golf than gambling. As Sam Orbaum, director of the Jerusalem club, has said on more than one occasion, "I always try to downplay this business of cheating. I act on it when I have to."

I recall an episode at the Western Championship in Reno in 1997. In a room with some 200 players the silence was broken by an agitated female voice. The woman was Karen Merrill, an expert player from Oregon. Her opponent was a man from Thailand. Merrill had been uneasy from the start of the match, because the man kept moving his hands to his lap. She decided to watch him. There was a point in the game, says Merrill, "when I couldn't believe my eyes." He brought a tile up from under the table with his right hand and put it on his rack, while at the same time he removed a tile from the other end of his rack with his left hand, which snaked its way back to his lap. Merrill yelled, "I want to see your hands!" "It was a gut reaction," she says. The miscreant wanted to put his hand in the tile bag, but Merrill told him not to move. Then she heard a clinking sound, like a tile hitting a metal chair leg. The director, Johnny Nevarez, came over. A tile was on the floor. Her opponent denied that he had done anything wrong. Still, Nevarez ended the game, which gave the victory to Merrill. The cheater wasn't caught dead to rights, so he was allowed to finish the tournament and slink home.

Player X, who would prefer to remain nameless, recently traveled to a Canadian event. Prior to one match he was warned about his opponent. "Watch him, he cheats," cautioned a friend who is a member of the same club as the alleged cheater. "For the first quarter of the game I was watching him, but then I got involved in my game and stopped," he says. He noticed that the alleged cheater did not raise the tile bag above eye level when drawing, something the tournament director emphasized that everyone had to do. Player X called him on it, but the alleged cheater said, "I can't do that," even though he had no apparent physical impairment.

The supposed cheater always drew with his thumb, index, and ring fingers, while cupping his other two fingers toward his body, a nice technique for dropping an unwanted tile back in the bag or for palming an extra one. In the end, X lost, while his opponent drew nine of the ten power tiles. "There's no doubt in my mind that he was palming," says X. "When I was watching him and wondering if he was palming tiles, yeah, it affected me mentally."

That's not the only way to gain an advantage, says Alice Van Luenen, an expert Oregon player. She knows of a California woman who has a special tile bag with a reinforced mouth that makes it always sit open. She places the bag on a stand that faces her, says Van Luenen, which allows her to peer in. Van Luenen doesn't have to play this woman because the scamp is in a lower division, but says, "I'm always kind of amazed at some of the things that players are allowed to get away with."

A woman showed up at a Florida tournament, says Susi Tiekert of Atlanta, toting her own bridge table and chairs. She insisted on using them because she said the regular chairs and tables were too high. At the end of the day some helpful young men volunteered to schlep her gear to the parking lot. They weren't prepared for what they found. On the underside of the table, right near the edge, the volunteers discovered a strip of two-way tape. "Undoubtedly," says Tiekert, "that was her seat position and the tape was used to squirrel away an occasional tile."

Cheating techniques are only limited by the ingenuity of the cheater. Susi Tiekert recalls a guy "who stuck a tile into the watch pocket of his jeans," and the ingenious way he was caught. In 1994 she was a word judge at the First Eastern Championship in Stamford, Connecticut. Charlie Southwell, of northern Virginia, was matched up against a guy we'll call Lee. Charlie suspected that Lee had palmed a tile. So he called over the director and asked that the tiles on the board and racks be counted.

The total came to ninety-nine, one short. Charlie then stood and turned his pockets inside out, says Tiekert. The director asked Lee to do the same. "Lee stood there like he was waiting for a bus," she says. "Finally, the director told Lee he was out of the tournament and Lee left the room." Although a complaint was filed with the NSA, there was talk of a lawsuit from Lee's side, so Lee was never banned from play.

Sam Orbaum of Jerusalem also has a cheating story. "A woman had been doing well at the Jerusalem club for many years," he says, "until I discovered that her tile bag had a hidden pocket, just big enough for two or three tiles, so she could draw a blank or an s when she needed one."

Orbaum crossed paths with another cheater in 1983 just after opening the doors of the Jerusalem club. Orbaum wrote for the *Jerusalem Post*, so as preparation for his club duties he had scoured the *Post*'s archives for Scrabble articles. One was a humorous piece on cheating techniques written by a well-known *Post* columnist who claimed to be quite a player. Well, the big day came, the club opened and Orbaum was pleased to find the columnist in attendance. She wasn't that good, but she became a regular. Then the complaints started: club members thought she was cheating. It turned out she was using the techniques she had described in her column.

Organized Scrabble doesn't have a systematic method for dealing with cheats. Hasbro fears lawsuits and doesn't want the NSA to take action unless the miscreant confesses or is caught so dead to rights that there is no room for discussion. Tournament directors are not crazy about getting involved, either. It's messy, confrontational, disrupts other players—and in the end it's difficult to make a case. At the same time, human monitors or videotaping to surveil play is too expensive and cumbersome. So the honest players whisper about cheats and try to keep one eye on their rack and the other on their opponent.

13

The Women

The Gender Disparity in Scrabble

Scrabble at the top is essentially a guy thing. Oh, there are excellent women players, and more women actually play competitive Scrabble than men, but at the apex of the game, guys rule. That may seem all wrong to the typical parlor player who believes the common perception that women tend to be more verbal and guys more mathematical. That could be part of the answer, since serious Scrabble is a game of probabilities that rewards those with mathematical rather than literary bents.

Twenty-five years ago there were more women at the top than there are today. At the 1978 North American Invitational, seven of the top thirty-two finishers were women. Four years later the February 1982 issue of *Scrabble Players Newspaper* devoted a page to women players. The headline was "The Year of the Women." Women were winning tournaments: Patti Morrison in

Birmingham, Alabama; Diane Pecnik in Lafayette, Louisiana; Ellis Wyer in Minneapolis, Minnesota; and Carol Clark in Mt. Airy, Pennsylvania.

Something has changed since those halcyon days. At the 2002 National Scrabble Championship held in San Diego, California, only three women—Pat Barrett, Robin Pollock Daniel, and Rita Norr—finished among the top thirty-two players. If we take a look at the Nationals in between, typically only one or two women placed in the top thirty-two, with a high of six in 1983 and a low of zero in 1992. These are telling numbers. Take the 2002 Nationals, where 687 of the letterati competed in six divisions. Here are the percentage of women in each division, from the experts in division one to the beginners in division six: 1) 14%, 2) 28%, 3) 57%, 4) 64%, 5) 64%, and 6) 69%. The women are concentrated in the bottom four divisions.

The national ratings tell a similar story. Of the top 100 players in 2002, only six were women: Robin Pollock Daniel, Pat Barrett, Rita Norr, Gail Wolford, Jan Dixon, and Lynn Cushman. What could account for this?

Robin Pollock Daniel has played on three Canadian World teams and posted a fifth-place finish in the 1995 Superstars. Daniel says it's not a question of ability, "Women are just socialized differently than men." Most girls are brought up to let the boys win, she says, learning "it's not attractive to beat a man." On top of that, they are told that what's important is to take care of a home or others "before we take care of ourselves," says Daniel, who has played less over recent years since becoming a mother herself.

"A lot of the top male players don't have lives beyond Scrabble," says Alice Van Luenen, an expert player from

Robin Pollock Daniel (L) and Luise Shafritz play partners in a pick-up game before the start of the 1996 Nationals in Dallas.

Oregon. "They are just totally obsessed with the game." She points to Joe Edley as an example. Back in the 1970s, he worked various odd jobs like night watchman and desk clerk so that he could devote himself to word study. "There is not a woman in the world who would be that obsessed with Scrabble," says Van Luenen.

Rita Norr, the only female winner of the Nationals, adds that women have to juggle homes, kids, and careers "and just don't have the time to study," whereas many of the top male players are single or don't have children. She adds, "Women don't have the killer instinct." And when they do, they apologize. Dennis Kaiser tells about getting beat twice by Karen Merrill, a strong Oregon player, at the 2002 Los Gatos tournament in California. The second loss knocked Kaiser out of the prize money and Merrill knew it. She looked across the table and apologized, says Kaiser. "Men just don't do that," he says. In fact, many would gloat.

Ann Sanfedele, who has been playing in New York City since the mid 1970s, says, "Men want to win more." They take the game more seriously and have a greater tendency than women to drop out if it becomes clear that they are destined for mediocrity. Luise Shafritz, of Las Vegas, has also observed this. Women can enjoy the game for the camaraderie and the travel, says Shafritz, something that she has seen much less of in men. Van Luenen points to testosterone as the causal agent. Women have been the mediators and the caregivers, she says, and the guys are supposed to go out and kill a mastodon. "Scrabble is another mastodon, and for most guys, if you don't kill it, it will kill you."

Jan Dixon, who placed fourth in the 1995 Superstars competition, contends that women's egos aren't as tied to their tournament performances as men's. What has accounted for her success? "I grew up with four brothers," says Dixon, "and learned to compete at an early age."

Another reason men may try harder, according to Van Luenen, is that many of them find it very difficult to lose to a woman. She and her former husband, Bob Schoenman, met through Scrabble and even played in the 1991 Thailand National Championship on their honeymoon. But the more they played at home, according to Van Luenen, the more losing to her became a problem for him. "There were periods when he refused to play me," she

Jean Carol and Gordon Shapiro at the 1989 Smoky
Mountain tournament in Gatlinburg, Tennessee.

says. She knows of some women who have thrown tournament games to avoid showing up their significant
others. "I'm not naming names because there might be
divorces," she says. "I don't think a guy would throw a
game like that in a gazillion years."

Women have another problem, according to Jean
Carol, who has been playing since the early 1980s. They
aren't being pushed by hard-charging young girls who

want to displace them. "Of the top ten women, I think six or seven of us played in the Boston Nationals in 1985," says Carol. "We don't have anyone like Joey Mallick [the then twenty-one-year-old Maine phenom] pressuring us."

Male explanations are all over the map too. One anonymous player thinks that men aren't necessarily smarter, but they tend to be better in those things that count in Scrabble—math and spatial relationship abilities, combined with a healthy dose of aggression and competitiveness. This guy doesn't accept the notion that women don't have as much time as men. He thinks men make the time.

Not all the top males are on the same page. Ron Tiekert thinks the main difference is competitive drive. Les Schonbrun thinks women aren't as driven to succeed at games because the culture discourages it; while at the same time "men are under pressure to be good at something." Brian Cappelletto sees the influence of culture too. "Gender doesn't really matter," he says, "but our culture still discourages women from excelling in the workplace and other competitive endeavors."

Susan Greendorfer is a sports psychologist in the Department of Kinesiology at the University of Illinois. She says, "Men are socialized to compete, while women are taught to cooperate. . . . Men don't consider women their equals, and women are socialized to believe that's true." This gives men an edge.

Carole Oglesby, a sports psychologist from Temple University, has done extensive research on female sports socialization. She also feels women have an uphill battle. In America, she says, winning is clearly a positive for males, but it often has a downside for females. Oglesby says this is particularly true when females vanquish males.

"There is a certain kind of social pain that goes along with that victory," she says. This could be relevant in Scrabble even if the woman is not aware of it, says Oglesby. "If one of the competitors is not single-minded about her focus and the benefits of winning," she says, "then that probably works against her."

This is an interesting theory, but what about reality? Carol Weisfeld, a psychologist at the University of Detroit, has studied girls in various mixed-gender competition situations, such as spelling bees, dodgeball, and mechanical problem solving. She has found that girls are much more competitive against one another than against boys. In fact, they tend to depress their performance against boys, says Weisfeld. There is no evidence that this is a conscious phenomenon. "There was a total lack of awareness," says Weisfeld. She sees it in evolutionary terms. Historically, men have competed for mates, while women sat back and chose the best performers. This is not something that changes overnight, she says. She would predict that in Scrabble, depressed performance would be most pronounced among women of childbearing age. "Women won't want to beat a guy who is a potential mate," she says, even if this is only a theoretical possibility. This may change after menopause, and Weisfeld thinks it would be fascinating to study the phenomenon in the Scrabble world. She suspects that once a woman's reproductive years have drawn to a close, she would become a more formidable opponent. "She might still be very attractive to men," says Weisfeld, "but her drive to reproduce would be over."

Psychologists have also looked at differences in brain functioning. Though no one knows what constitutes the optimal Scrabble brain, men tend to perform better in mathematical reasoning tests, an aptitude often cited as important to the game. Doreen Kimura, of Simon Fraser University in Vancouver, says, "Men outnumber women at the upper end of the SAT math scores and also do better on very abstruse math exams." Kimura, who is the author of *Sex and Cognition*, also points out that women make up a very small percentage of math, physics, and engineering faculties, which she attributes to the math differential. The one advantage that women have, which would help in Scrabble, is a greater ability than men to memorize and recall word lists. "Men score better on tests of spatial relationships, three-dimensional mental rotations, and block design," says Irwin Silverman, an evolutionary psychologist at York University in Toronto. While all these skills can be improved, and Silverman suspects playing Scrabble would do that, he thinks the average woman would still lag behind the average man. These skills and their development, however, are tied to the socialization and education women and men receive, so it's difficult to determine whether these test scores reflect an innate biological difference between the genders or a difference in their upbringing—the age-old nature versus nurture debate.

Of course, anyone who wants to excel at Scrabble has to give up a chunk of his or her life and some people think that doesn't mesh well with the interests of young women. Devoting endless hours to working LeXpert racks on a computer screen or memorizing word lists strikes Carole Oglesby as the last thing that would interest a girl. Girls and women tend to choose sports that are more social than males do, according to Linda Bunker, who is in the Department of Kinesiology at the University of Virginia. "Girls have a greater tendency to play in order to have fun

Lisa Odom shows Robin Pollock Daniel her winning board in
the last game of the 2004 Nationals in New Orleans. Lisa
came in 21st of 173 with an 18–11 record, the highest-
finishing woman in the tournament.

and be in a social group, not to compete," says Bunker.
Weisfeld adds that competitive Scrabble is just too iso-
lating for most girls. "I think where you tend to find girls
totally focusing themselves is in gymnastics, dance, music,
or team sports where they can work with other people,"
she says. These academics, then, wouldn't expect many
girls to be interested in serious Scrabble, and for those that
do get involved, their mathematical reasoning skills, if
lacking, could get in the way of high achievements.

Are the women who do participate in competitive
Scrabble welcomed in the androgen-drenched atmosphere
at the top of the game? Rita Norr thinks that some women
who rise to a certain skill level expect to lose, but is quick
to add that "the better women players are not intimidated
by any of these guys." Are they accepted? Norr says she

doesn't have any problems, but thinks it's because she has played for many years. New female players might find it more difficult to fit in, she says.

Robin Pollock Daniel recalls that when she began playing tournaments it seemed as if there were just two groups. There was Joe Edley and Ron Tiekert, and then there was everybody else. "It was a 'Mr. Edley, can I have your autograph?' kind of atmosphere," she says. But that has changed, as the general caliber of all players has improved, says Daniel. "So I think the top guys have softened a bit," she says. Acceptance has never been a problem for her. She hasn't been excluded and "I never had any male crap thrown my way, either." Van Luenen isn't so sure that social acceptance is high on most female players' wish lists. She knows that going out to dinner to analyze the day's games doesn't interest her, and yet she realizes that's what many of the men do. She is more interested, she says, in getting to know the players as people and not as Scrabble players, and thinks most women would agree. Daniel isn't anticipating a glut of women entering the competitive Scrabble world. "I think boys like to play and they always will," she says, "while women can take it or leave it."

14

Beginnings and Endings

Prodigies and Retirees

A common misconception held by parlor players is that age goes hand in hand with vocabulary. It stands to reason that a person who has lived longer, read more, and has probably had more education will have more words under her belt. That's generally true when talking about everyday language—the words that we know and can use in conversation, or can define on demand. But it's a mistake to extend this generalization to Scrabble, where serious players study word lists and prodigies are not uncommon. Take Nick Ballard.

Nick Ballard hasn't played seriously since his retirement in 1994, as the fifth-ranked player in North America. Back in 1975, at age seventeen, Ballard learned the game at the knee of Lester Schonbrun in Oakland, California. "Lester was a guru to me," says Ballard. He would beeline it to Schonbrun's house after school to play for a penny or two a point. "I considered these very cheap lessons," says Ballard.

Schonbrun regularly gave him anagrammatic problems as homework. He once asked Ballard to work out the anagrams for ACENORSTU, which was no small matter, since it involved rummaging through the entire dictionary. "Hunting through *Funk & Wagnalls*, I found COURANTES, OUTRANCES, NECTAROUS, and COURTESAN," says Ballard. "I didn't know of any other promising players my age in the mid 1970s." If they existed, they probably switched to another game that required less research. What is child's play today with a PDA or desktop computer required real commitment on the part of the up-and-coming player back then.

Ballard learned quickly. When he moved to Chicago in 1978 at the age of twenty, he won most of the tournaments he entered. In 1979, he flew to New York City with John Ozag and won a tournament at the Game Room. In Chicago he honed his skills against Bob Felt, who went on to win the Nationals in 1990.

In 1989 Ballard began publishing *Medleys*, considered the best Scrabble newsletter ever. From 1991–93 Ballard produced the monthly, often putting in sixteen-hour days. Its audience was the 250 or so top players. He couldn't make a living from it. In *Medleys*, Ballard and Charlie Carroll popularized anamonics, a method for ordering and recalling seven- and eight-letter words composed from six- and seven-letter stems.

In the 1980s, teenager Brian Cappelletto was considered a prodigy. He started playing with his family at age seven. At eleven he graduated to games with neighbor Jim Wait, a mid-level tournament player. By age fifteen he was

Brian Cappelletto playing in the 1991 Boston Area
Tournament premier division.

ready for the Phoenix Scrabble club. The following year, in
October 1985, he went 5–5 in his first tournament in
Albuquerque, New Mexico. In January 1986 he captured
his first win (9–1) in Mesa, Arizona.

While in high school, Cappelletto played with the late
Stan Rubinsky, a seasoned tournament goer. "He was the
biggest influence I had early on," says Cappelletto. He
also got plenty of help from his mother. She encouraged

him, paid for his trips to out-of-town events, and let him keep his winnings. One time, when the flight from Phoenix to Durango, Colorado, was cancelled, she drove 400 miles through the night so that he could play in the Durango tournament the next morning.

Cappelletto had natural talent but he worked at it too. "This stuff doesn't just happen overnight," he says. At one point he got Mike Baron's *Bingo Book*, and flashcarded all the seven- and eight-letter words he didn't know, sometimes putting in two or three hours a day. The project took two years. "There was a period of time," he says, "when Scrabble was on my mind every waking second. Nothing else mattered."

He rose quickly, winning twenty-one tournaments in his first six years of play, placed second in the first World Championship in 1991, then won the Nationals in 1998 and the Worlds in 2001. At age thirty-two, he had sixteen years of tournament experience under his belt.

It's difficult to think of Adam Logan as a prodigy, but that is what he was. He has already won the 1996 National Scrabble Championship, the 1996 Canadian Nationals, and the 2005 Worlds, but he is only in his early thirties.

Logan got a fast start. He began playing with his mother at age seven, then tried a tournament against adults when just shy of his tenth birthday, where he sat on a telephone book to get a proper view of the board. He liked bridge and still does, but it was easier to get into serious Scrabble (you only need two people, not four) so he switched allegiances. At thirteen he chalked up his first intermediate division win. At fourteen he adopted a study program, which took time away from his other consuming interest—mathematics. Logan added an hour of word

Ann Sanfedele gets a hug from the 1996 National champ,
Adam Logan, just after he won.

work each day to a regimen that already included playing
against both humans and computers. "Even when I wasn't
playing or studying," says Logan, "I'd often just happen
to think of anagrams, or plays I could have made in recent
games." In 1988 he bagged his first expert division win at
a tournament in Hamilton, Ontario. He was fifteen and
one of Canada's best players.

Logan was also busy with other things. He graduated
from high school at sixteen, finished Princeton in mathematics at twenty, and obtained his Ph.D. in mathematics
from Harvard at twenty-four. This didn't leave a lot of
time for Scrabble.

He did play, but he didn't travel to tournaments as
much as he would have liked. He studied mostly in the

summer. It wasn't so much the lack of time, he says now, as it was the lack of energy and the ability to concentrate. "When you've spent three or four hours puzzling over a difficult math book," says Logan, "it's very hard to get yourself to study words."

An aspect of the game he relishes is what he calls "swindles." These are ways to win games near their end when they appear lost. He recalls an example from a recent club match where his opponent had the game won if she made proper use of the z. But it was Logan's turn. He knew her tiles because this was the final rack of the game and he had tracked the tiles played to that point. He saw the move she should make to set up an unstoppable z play on her next turn. "So I made another spot where she could play BAIZE for fewer points," says Logan. "She took the bait and lost."

Today there are several dozen players under the age of eighteen who play serious Scrabble. This contrasts starkly with the 1970s when Nick Ballard may have been alone: why? The top players in the 1970s studied the dictionary and compiled word lists, but most tournament players didn't. It was a chore. Most people considered Scrabble a literary game based on natural vocabulary and education, things that took many years to acquire. Serious Scrabble, then, was an adult game. With the advent of word lists, along with the realization by most tournament players that study was the key to success, all that changed. Natural vocabulary took a backseat to memorizing letter strings. Then came computers in the mid 1980s. Electronic study aids like LeXpert and V-Flash followed, which gave a new twist to studying and made list generation a snap. It was no longer a question of one's education, or even one's commitment to scouring the dictionary. It became a matter of one's willingness to make the time to memorize the words—something a bright teen could do.

Getting to the top of the Scrabble world requires many years of play and study. Yet, once there, some of the letterati have turned around and retired, long before their best playing days were over. The question is why. Scrabble is a high maintenance game. It requires a heavy study commitment, one that never ends. Words are added or subtracted from the lexicon. Keeping up is hard. David Prinz found that out twenty-five years ago.

He won the North American Invitational in 1978 and finished fifth in 1980. Then he opened a music store in the San Francisco Bay area. Suddenly he had no time. He dropped out rather than embarrass himself with sub par outings. In his prime, though, he knew a lot of words. After all, he had been one of the primary compilers of the *Official Scrabble Players Dictionary*. But he admits a lot of that has faded away. He'd like to play again, but getting back in shape "looks like too much work," he says. Prinz thinks he could do it if he wanted to. "It's probably the thing I did best in the world," he says. He doesn't want to play, though, unless he can win, and there is the matter of the words. On top of that, he feels, the top players don't have lives and there's no money in it. (Though he admits that, yes, he only played for the glory anyway.) Maybe when he retires he'll give it another go: "I still think that if I got back into studying I could win the Nationals," he says.

Peter Morris, of Michigan, is another former star who is a bit short on words. He won the National Scrabble Championship in 1989 and the first World Championship in 1991, but retired not long afterward. Morris says that

Bob Watson, back to camera, versus Peter Morris in the
1988 Nationals in Reno. This is the penultimate game.

he did most of his studying in 1984 and 1985 and that it
held him in good stead for some seven years. But a number
of things happened in 1992 that convinced him it was time
to hang up his racks. To begin with he began to forget
words he once knew. Then, the revised edition of the
Official Scrabble Players Dictionary came out—more new
words. And he found himself inadvertently playing some
of the British words he had learned for the Worlds. So he
needed to refresh his old word knowledge, learn some new
words, and forget the British words. "I couldn't do that,"
says Morris. "Oh, maybe if I had been willing to put in the
time, but I wasn't." Rather than play at a level that he felt
was beneath him, Morris retired. Would he come back? "I
would never say never," says Morris, who today works as

a copy editor and writes books on the history of baseball.

Another fallen-away champion is David Gibson. The 1994 Nationals winner, who also took the prestigious 1995 Superstars in Las Vegas, was, until recently, happy to teach math at Spartanburg Methodist College in South Carolina and write songs with his wife, Nancy. In his heyday he studied 17,000 flashcards regularly, even learned the meanings of the words. "The rigors of keeping up were a big factor in my retirement," he says, after he had been at it four to five hours a day for ten years. "I knew what it took to get there and I knew what it would take to stay there," he says. "I needed a break."

It had been roughly seven years since Gibson chucked out his flashcards. For five of those years he didn't play a game. Then, he played a few games with his wife. He followed them with several sessions with Randy Hersom, an expert North Carolina player. Is he coming back? A non-committal Gibson responds, "I could play again, then, maybe not." Yet, in the spring of 2002, there he was at a tournament in Gatlinburg, Tennessee. In August he played in the San Diego Nationals. In 2003 he ended all speculation with a convincing win at the televised All-Stars Tournament, pocketing the $50,000 first prize. He followed that with a second-place finish at the 2004 Nationals. Gibson is back.

Someone who is truly retired is Stephen Fisher. He was the top-rated player in Canada throughout the 1980s and played on the 1991 Canadian World team, before retirement at age forty-three. During his glory days Fisher maintained a rating of roughly 2050, but found it grueling. Then he too was confronted with the revised *Official Scrabble Players Dictionary*. "I couldn't handle the thought of starting over," he says. And in a comment all too similar to those made by older athletes who have lost a step, he says, "My memory wasn't working anywhere near as well as it had, either." He got married in 1985 and bought a house; he says, "It's hard to maintain your Scrabble and a normal life." So he quit and took up cycling, roller blading, and skiing. What would it take to bring him back? "Reconnected synapses would be a big start," says Fisher, "but I really don't want the stress anymore."

Some people, though, have retired to make a point. Perhaps Nick Ballard, of San Francisco, is the best example. He was a top player in the 1980s and played on the World team in 1993. But Ballard was an early advocate of SOWPODS, the combining of the North American *Official Scrabble Players Dictionary* and the British *Official Scrabble Words*. When SOWPODS didn't happen, he retired. Today Ballard says that there was more to it than that. He wanted to make a living from the game. "I have always made my living at games in one way or another," says the number-one ranked backgammon player in the world. Nothing would bring him back.

The word source also helped to drive Dan Pratt, of Baltimore, out of the game. Pratt, a government mathematician, finished no worse than fifth in the first four Nationals, and in 1981 single-handedly got the Scrabble rating system off the ground. He was never a fan of the *Official Scrabble Players Dictionary*. He retired in 1991, came back, then retired again in 1995, but still periodically attends a local club to see old friends. "I don't want to play with an out-of-whack word source," says Pratt, who feels that a conversion to SOWPODS would make the

Dan Pratt, of Baltimore, shows Mike Wise, of Canada, that
the settings on the analog clock are correct, a part of the
ritual at a tournament before the use of digital clocks
became standard.

situation even worse. Even so, in the past two years the
lure of the tiles has proved too much. Crummy lexicon or
not, Pratt is back.

Another protest retirement came from a young Brian
Cappelletto. In August 1993, he retired, at the grand old
age of twenty-one. He wasn't happy with the divisional
cutoffs at the Nationals, which permitted high mid-level
players to compete with the elite. Nor did he like the qualifying method for the World Championship. These and
other things suggested to Cappelletto that Hasbro didn't
value the pursuit of excellence in tournament Scrabble.

Then a funny thing happened. In 1995 Hasbro put on

the Superstars Tournament for the top fifty rated players, with $100,000 in prize money—$50,000 of which would go to the winner. This was enough for Cappelletto. He came back. "The Superstars demonstrated a higher level of commitment," he says. "The game is better now than when I retired."

It takes a special sort of person to play at the top and stay there. Cappelletto thinks it's a balancing act. "Some people just aren't able to juggle Scrabble with family and work," he says. Bob Lipton, of Vero Beach, Florida, who is usually among the top fifty letterati, agrees. He knows that some players have dropped out at all levels because of a lack of spousal support, but Lipton, who recently married, says, "I made sure I picked a mate who would be supportive." He doesn't see burnout as a problem, either. He says he loves to study. Even so, Lipton has recently admitted to being in "temporary retirement," but as of April 2008, has plans to play in the Texas SOWPODS Challenge Tournament.

Les Schonbrun, of Oakland, California, isn't going anywhere, either. He may be in his early seventies, but he's usually in the top fifty players in North America and having fun. He sometimes feels the strain of the game and wonders "whether my bladder and other systems can stand it. But the fun of competing outweighs all that." He hates to lose and if it became a regular occurrence, he might consider retirement. "But the great thing about Scrabble is that you can always pretend your poor performances were bad luck, and for that matter, maybe they were."

One thing that would have kept some of these players active, and even today might get some of them back in the game, is money. In other sports and games, where the top performers can earn a living, they seldom retire before their time. To the contrary, they often play longer than they should. Making a living from Scrabble isn't an option. If it were, that might change the whole complexion of the game.

15

Then and Now

Evolution of the Game

The history of organized Scrabble reflects a constantly evolving game. Competitive players as a whole are far better today than they were in 1973 or, for that matter, in 1993. Some of this improvement can be attributed to the maturation of the players, but at the root of the improvement is a more systematic approach to the game.

Prior to 1973, the year Selchow & Righter organized tournament and club Scrabble, almost everyone who played was a parlor player. The exceptions were in the New York game rooms. If you asked what it took to be good, they would have cited things like a large vocabulary, a good education, and a background in English.

In the early 1970s there was an inkling of what was to come. Mike Senkiewicz along with Les Schonbrun were considered the best players in New York. Senkiewicz was rumored to have memorized the *Funk & Wagnalls*

Dictionary and he also made word lists, which he shared. So it made sense for Selchow & Righter to put Senkiewicz on the payroll as a consultant in 1972. When Scrabble Crossword Game Players began publication of the *Scrabble Players Newspaper*, he wrote a column on Scrabble strategy.

As early as the second issue, in the fall of 1973, Senkiewicz talked about the SATIRE stem. "A number of years ago," he wrote, "the best New York players found a rack of six tiles that provided the greatest possibility of playing a bingo [a seven-letter word] with any seventh tile." Eighteen letters of the alphabet accomplished this feat. He asked readers to find as many of those seven-letter words as they could. Senkiewicz provided the word list and no doubt players from coast to coast got their first realization of a more sophisticated approach to the game. One didn't have to be educated, middle aged, or a big reader. It was just a matter of wanting to learn to play. That original SATIRE list consisted of thirty-four words, far short of the seventy on it today.

About this time Senkiewicz also came out with the *Scrabble Players Handbook*. This Selchow & Righter publication was the first in a short list of how-to Scrabble books. Somewhat primitive by today's standards, it still contained sections on rack balancing, strategy, and bluffing, and surely got thousands of people to think about how they could improve their play. The book made it clear that Scrabble could be learned like algebra, French, or cooking.

Meanwhile the *Scrabble Players Newspaper* published more stems, with their associated lists of seven-letter words. The SANTER list appeared in 1974, followed by the

SETTER, SENDER, and SALTER stems in 1975, and the ENTERS and ASSERT stems in 1976. The same year Scrabble Crossword Game Players made these lists available for a stamped self-addressed envelope. Scrabble was changing.

Jim Pate, an Alabama player, created the SALTER stem. He recalls that he first took promising sets of six letters, added a letter, and tried to find as many seven-letter words as he could. If the number of usable seventh letters reached sixteen, he made a systematic search of the entire *Funk & Wagnalls*. It took him a month on and off to finish the SALTER stem. "Boy, did I feel like I had discovered something big," says Pate. And he had. There were fifty words.

A none
B blaster, labrets
C cartels, clarets, crestal, scarlet
D dartles
E relates, stealer, elaters, realest
F falters
G largest
H halters, lathers, slather, thalers, harslet
I saltier, saltire, retails, slatier, realist
J none
K talkers, stalker
L stellar
M armlets
N antlers, sternal, rentals, saltern
O none
P psalter, plaster, platers, palters, stapler, persalt
Q none
R none
S salters, artless, lasters, slaters

T rattles, startle, starlet
U saluter, estrual
V varlets, travels
W wastrel, warstle
X none
Y none
Z none

His work was far from the last word on stems, though. The letterati continued to create them. One of the implications of these lists was that good players studied. Certainly, many of the words in the SALTER list were familiar, like BLASTER, FALTERS, or STARTLE. But what about CRESTAL, HARSLET, and PSALTER? Most people wouldn't have known them, even though the constituent letters were very likely to come up on their racks. No doubt many new club players reasoned that if they wanted to stay competitive, they had better begin studying.

The *Official Scrabble Players Dictionary* was the next big step. Since some time in the 1960s when the Fleahouse crowd had decided to make *Funk & Wagnalls* their word source, that dictionary had caught on. But because *Funk & Wagnalls* was a real dictionary, it was not ideal for adjudicating word disputes.

When the *Official Scrabble Players Dictionary* (OSPD) came along in 1978, all that changed. It increased the size of the acceptable lexicon. It meant that the old-timers had some retooling to do and that those who wanted to dig into the game had a much more usable word source from which to work. Paul Avrin recalls that a number of players dropped out rather than deal with the new book. Others, like Joe Edley and Jerry Lerman in San Francisco, saw it as an opportunity to learn the game.

The new dictionary had its critics, but despite its terse definitions, misprints, and obviously foreign words, it had many advantages. All the words were in alphabetical order. All the plurals and comparatives were given. There was no guesswork. A player didn't have to be an accomplished dictionary user to find what she was looking for. The *Official Scrabble Players Dictionary* was more portable because the definitions were short and the volume was limited to words of eight letters or less. It was also more list-like and easier to study than a standard dictionary.

Then came probability thinking. Today all the top players take for granted that Scrabble is a game of probabilities. Maybe some of the better players engaged in rudimentary probability calculations prior to 1980, but it was left to Al Weissman, a Connecticut player and neuropharmacologist, to write about probability for the first time in the *Scrabble Players Newspaper* in February 1980.

Weissman had played chess in his teens and read strategy tomes. When he moved over to Scrabble as an adult, he wanted to do something to remedy its lack of how-to literature. In his seminal article, "Some Scrabble Game Mathematics," he laid out the probability of drawing various racks of seven tiles and concluded, "the best bonus words [seven-letter words] to memorize are those formed from the most common letters." In other words, one-point tiles were the most likely tiles to produce seven-letter words. In the same issue, word mavens Joe Leonard, David Shulman, and Jack Marquis published a list of the most potent six-letter stems, like Jim Pate's SALTER. The message was clear: anyone who planned to study seven- or eight-letter words would make the most efficient use of his time with these lists because they contained the words that were the most likely to come up in random draws.

This approach probably went over the heads of many players, and didn't interest others, but it allowed many to see the game in a new light. It permitted the novice as well as the expert to think in terms of which letters it made the most sense to save and which others to immediately play off. What might have made intuitive sense to some of the better players, now had a grounding in probability. Scrabble was becoming less about being literate and more about being numerate.

By the mid 1980s the stage was set for someone to do a computer analysis of the *Official Scrabble Players Dictionary* and that person was Mike Baron, an Albuquerque, New Mexico, psychologist. There were already some extensive word lists, beyond the SALTER type. Most notably, a multi-volume set of the sevens and eights, produced by Joel Lipman of Maryland, which sold for fifty dollars. And a similar list of large print sevens and eights hawked by Charles Goldstein of Berkeley, California, for $500. "I had a few takers," says Goldstein. It was left to Mike Baron, though, to produce the ultimate book of lists.

He likes to tell the story of how it all started. He was matched up against Charles Goldstein in a regional qualifying event for the 1980 North American Invitational. Goldstein played KNUR and to his chagrin, Baron challenged and lost. "I didn't want that to happen again," says Baron, "so I began compiling word lists from the *Official Scrabble Players Dictionary*."

Baron's lists, which he often compiled with Joe

Charles Goldstein accepting fifth-place money from Johnny
Navarez at the 1995 Western Championship in Reno.

Leonard, of Philadelphia, appeared in the *Scrabble Players
Newspaper* from 1980 through 1987. Baron began with
the two letter words, which with the addition of one letter
could make a three. AA, for example, could morph to BAA,
AAH, AAL, or AAS. This list came out in 1981 and in a
slightly revised form is what newcomers receive at their
first Scrabble club sessions even today.

Many other hand-generated lists followed. The most
important list, initially hand-generated, was the 100 most
probable six-letter stems, like SALTER. Baron built on the
probability thinking of Al Weissman, as well as the stem
concept already kicking around and the earlier work done
by Joe Leonard. In addition, he refined our understanding

of which seven- and eight-letter words were, in probability terms, worth learning, or at least made the most sense to learn first, if a player wanted to get the most bang from her study-time buck.

This began as a labor intensive, page-by-page struggle to extract gold from the *Official Scrabble Players Dictionary*, but toward the end computers came to the rescue. First, Jim Lamerand put the dictionary in machine-readable form. In 1985 this allowed Baron to generate a velo-bound list, the *Bingo Book*, of all the seven and eights at the bargain price of six dollars.

In 1988 Baron and Jere Guin, a programmer, published *The Wordbook*, which consisted of some 300 pages of small-print word lists. The initial print run of 300 copies was shipped directly to Reno for the 1988 Nationals. "I just hoped I wouldn't have to ship any back to New Mexico," says Baron. And he didn't.

The notion of Scrabble as a vocabulary game for the literate and well-read had been under attack for some time. There were no formal skirmishes but a few people, like Dan Pratt and the late Milt Wertheimer, longed for the old days when more people knew the meanings of the words that they played. But the era of word lists had arrived. *The Wordbook* had no definitions, just page after page of lists. The subtext was obvious; if you wanted to win, memorize.

Someone who did this was Brian Cappelletto, who in 1985, at age fifteen, made his tournament debut. He had discovered Baron's *Bingo Book* and learned it. He says that not everyone was as excited about learning word lists as he was, and that there was even a backlash of sorts. In the early 1990s, when he was already a top player, he says there was a great deal of resentment toward people like himself who had memorized the lists and taken the game further than it had ever gone before. "Top players were often disparaged and resented, and rarely acknowledged for their great play," says Cappelletto. There was a tendency to dwell on their personal eccentricities and claim that they didn't have lives.

Still, the word list juggernaut rolled on. Many players, even if they wanted to learn the lists, found that it wasn't easy to keep them straight. So at about the same time as *The Wordbook* appeared in Reno, some 300 miles to the south in Las Vegas, a croupier, named Bob Lipton, was experimenting with a system to solve that problem. It would eventually become known as anamonics. It enabled the high level player to mentally juggle more words than ever before and to recall them more easily.

There are various approaches to anamonics, but the basic idea is to help players remember which letters combine with six-letter stems like SALTER to form seven- or eight-letter words. This technique is not used by all the best players, but those who have adopted it, swear by it. An example might help here.

Since 1975 when Jim Pate produced his SALTER stem, thousands of others have been developed. Yet, if a player finds one of these stems on his rack, what then? Let's consider TISANE, which is the strongest and most common stem. It will combine with twenty-three letters of the alphabet to form 69 seven-letter words from ACETINS to ZEATINS. But which twenty-three? Lipton associated a phrase with each stem. Each unique letter in the phrase (there are twenty-three) combines with the stem to form at least one seven-letter word. In the case of TISANE, which is a tea, the phrase is "Makes Excellent Herb Tea, Giving Food A Powerful Buzz." So TISANE plus an M results in ETAMINS, INMATES, and TAMEINS, while TISANE plus a Z is ZANIEST or ZEATINS. Anamonic enthusiasts commit hundreds, or even thousands of these phrases to memory. Anamonics also help to spot phony words. If a word contains a stem, but none of the letters in the anamonic, it's a phony.

A	entasia, taenias
B	banties, basinet
C	acetins, cineast
D	destain, detains, instead, nidates, sainted, stained
E	etesian
F	fainest
G	easting, eatings, ingates, ingesta, seating, teasing
H	sheitan, sthenia
I	isatine
J	none
K	intakes
L	elastin, entails, nailset, salient, saltine, slainte, tenails
M	etamins, inmates, tameins
N	inanest, stanine
O	atonies
P	panties, patines, sapient, spinate
Q	none
R	anestri, antsier, nastier, ratines, retains, retinas, retsina, stainer, stearin
S	entasis, seitans, tansies, nasties, sestina, tisanes
T	instate, satinet
U	aunties, sinuate
V	naivest, natives, vainest
W	tawnies, waniest
X	antisex, sextain

Y   none
Z   zaniest, zeatins

Just as probability had nudged serious players out of the parlor where most Americans played, anamonics propelled them even further from the mainstream of American tile pushers. Not only were word definitions considered unimportant, but a wholly artificial structure was superimposed on the lexicon—an artificial structure that even many lower-level tournament players knew nothing about, and still don't.

Anamonics was not the only new force impinging on the game. The computer was about to enable people to play, study, and strategize as never before. Every man could be his own Baron, so to speak. Various computer programs for both play and study have been around since the late 1980s. They have made it possible for the Scrabble obsessed to play more games in a day than they often play against humans in a month. But one program took the game to the next strategic level.

It's called Maven. Developed by Brian Sheppard, a Boston area programmer, Maven took the top players by storm when it appeared on the Mac in 1986. Maven played so well, that some players thought it was cheating. What started for Sheppard in 1983 as an intellectual exercise to improve on a Scrabble program he had seen in a technical computing journal, turned into a thirteen-year quest, that saw Maven evolve into the almost perfect across-the-board adversary. "It basically blew everyone off the board," says Sheppard, including Joe Edley, Jim Neuberger, Chris Cree, and Bob Felt. Maven was such a hit that some players bought Macs just so they could run it.

Trey Wright, back to camera, just beat Chris Cree to advance
to the best-of-five round at the 2004 Nationals in New
Orleans. Cree has a stiff upper lip while Marlon Hill offers
comfort. It was a heartbreaking loss for Cree. Wright went
on win the whole thing.

Sheppard had few preconceived notions about how to
play. He thought about each rack of tiles as assets, some
good and some bad. He wanted to see how he could play
off the bad tiles, at the same time as he saved the good
ones, and in the process maximize the number of points
scored. "So I wrote down the equations that best
described that kind of system," he says. He discussed the

project with Bob Felt and Peter Morris, who would win the first Worlds in 1991. "I started out thinking that Brian was going to learn a lot from me," says Morris, "but I think I learned more from him."

Many players maximized tile turnover. They played long words in an effort to draw the blanks and Ss. Maven proved that was a mistake, when it resulted in breaking up racks of synergistic tiles like TAIN or TERS, for just a few points, since that reduced the chances of forming a seven- or eight-letter word on the next turn. Some people also played very defensively. They tried to limit their opponent's scoring and in the process reduced their own. Maven showed that was a mistake too.

There were other revelations, but perhaps the most important feature of the program was the simulator. Often times it isn't clear which move is the best to make. Back in the early 1980s Ron Tiekert was the first player to experiment with hand simulation. He set up positions, drew for both sides, and recorded the results—120 times. He once simmed the opening rack of AAADERW. He found that AWA was the best move by far, some eight points better than the other choices, even though DRAW or AWARD might be the first picks in the minds of some players. The reason for AWA was the nice leave of ADER.

Enter Maven. With Maven's simulator, which incorporates all the strategy and tactics used to play a game, the program can examine a particular move or moves to see which one scores the most in the short run, or it can actually play out tens of thousands of simulated games, to determine which move leads to the most wins in the long run. Simulation allowed the top players to look at strategic alternatives in ways that they never had before.

Recently, a group of MIT players have superseded Maven with Quackle, an even better program.

There are also computer word-study programs. The two most prominent ones are LeXpert, developed by M. G. Ravichandran, and Video-Flashcards, developed by Robert Parker. Both programs produce electronic flash-cards. They contain both predefined lists of words—for example, the 1000 most-probable sevens—and they can generate any imaginable list—for example, three-vowel sevens or all the eights ending in -INGS. The user can study these lists by manipulating the tiles on screen or can print paper versions. Recently, Michael Thelen has improved on these programs with Zyzzyva.

But that's not all that computing has contributed to the organized game. People both play online and gather online to discuss the game. They play at the International Scrabble Club, which is located on a server in Romania. They keep in touch at Scrabble Crossword Game Pro (CGP), a listserv where players who are NSA members can discuss Scrabble-related issues and pass along the latest Scrabble gossip. It was started at MIT in 1994, is run by Sherrie Saint John, and resides on Yahoo. It's a place where top players can kick around issues and neophytes can ask questions.

These changes have not gone unnoticed. Jerry Lerman says there are a lot fewer word lovers in the game than when he started out in the 1970s. He probably has mixed emotions about that because when he moved over from the tense environment of tournament chess, the relative tranquility of the Scrabble world allowed him to coast. But no more. People are more competitive and intense than they were in the old days, says Lerman. "Back then I was playing against people who loved words more than they loved to win."

Les Schonbrun has noticed this too. There was much less studying in the old days, so players didn't know as many words. But with the advent of handheld electronic dictionaries, computer-generated lists, and electronic studying, this has all changed. "Even ten years ago," says Schonbrun, "it was far less common to find people who knew the threes, fours, and fives and lists of the common sevens and eights. Today it's assumed."

In the old days seven- and eight-letter words were the province of the best players, while now even most mid-level players have a large arsenal of these words. According to the late Bob Felt, "This makes stealing games from opponents who severely out-tile you [draw better than you do] much more difficult that it was fifteen years ago."

Every game is chancier for the top players, according to Schonbrun. There are fewer slam-dunk games, even if over the long haul, the better players end up near the top of the tournament standings. "The landscape has changed," says Florida's Bob Lipton. "The 200th best player might win a tournament that ten years ago would have been the exclusive province of the elite top fifty. Parity has arrived."

16

Life at the Top

What It Takes To Be Good

If you've read this far you are probably wondering what it takes to become a good player. You aren't alone. Anyone who takes more than a casual interest in the game can't help but speculate. As it turns out, many tangible and intangible things play a role, and even the top letterati disagree about which factors are most important. That said, we can talk to the experts and get some opinions.

No one just sits down at the board and intuitively knows how to play well; some people have more aptitude than others; some see more quickly what needs to be done to improve. But the game has to be learned. A meteoric rise might take three or four years, but most players require six, eight, or even ten years to get to the top.

Some people don't have the gray matter to play at the highest levels. The first year or two of serious competition and study can be deceiving because enormous strides are possible. Each new word list, strategy tip, or anagramming breakthrough provides immediate payoffs. Your scores improve; you play more bingos per game; and you win more. Family and friends can't beat you. Still, after a couple of years, those new seven- and eight-letter words aren't coming up that often, which is logical, because they aren't as probable as the TISANE and SATIRE racks that initially goosed your game into gear; they contain more high-point and duplicate tiles. Then you begin to notice that you've forgotten words that you once played, maybe even challenge one now and then.

Some people's memories are better than others. The game is like that. It has a way of reminding you of your limitations. A rack comes up that you recognize, but try as you might, you can't tease out the word. Is INSURANT spelled with an I or an E? Does ZLOTE take an S or doesn't it? These and many other questions constantly rear their heads. As time passes, there are fewer mistakes than there once were, but still more than the better players make.

The realization that I didn't have that special combination of mental skills that makes a top player hit me about four years ago. I didn't have high expectations at the start, but my rating rose rapidly, and so did my optimism. But that rating hovered in the 1600s (nothing to be ashamed of) for three years, despite my increased word knowledge and strategic awareness. I was stuck. Only after the 2004 Nationals did I dribble over 1700.

This makes it more difficult to keep up a study regimen, which I now seem to slip in and out of. There's a feeling of "what's the use?" I've improved but so has everyone else. My increments of growth are so small now that they go all but unnoticed. I can't be great, but I can be better—the tortoise, not the hare.

So what keeps people like me at it? Scrabble fills a void. Bagging it is not an option. I can't play for fun either. I plod on, with a little voice in the back of my head saying that maybe some day, with enough repetition, the words will stick, the strategy will bloom, the anagramming will improve, and I'll be pretty damned good. Maybe. In the meantime, what is it that makes those other players so good?

No one has studied it, but certainly the top players are bright and it's probably safe to say the brighter the better. A number, for example, report SAT scores in the 1500s (out of 1600), with math scores over 700. While all sorts of professions are found among the top fifty players, there is an over-representation of math and computer types, which suggests that analytical thinkers are best suited to the game. Adam Logan, of Ottawa, a mathematician who won the 1996 National Championship at the age of twenty-two, has a theory about this. He thinks such people have a greater willingness "to learn arbitrary information." What he means is that they have studied languages, both computer and mathematical, where first they learned the rules (the syntax) without any associated meaning and only later picked up the context of those rules (the semantics), or the meaning. This is analogous to what serious Scrabble players do. The words are mastered, for the most part, without meanings. The math and computer types are comfortable doing this. They aren't so much learning words as they are the rules of the game— the syntax. The fledgling player, to the contrary, is often heard to say, "I can't learn these words if I don't know what they mean." Not Logan. "It seems to me," he says, "that some people [non-math types] often want to under-stand everything, which can be a real hindrance."

The math and computer folks have also studied proba-bility theory. And Scrabble is a game of probabilities. Players don't calculate the odds before every move, but there are times when having a rough idea of the chances of drawing a particular tile, or your opponent's chances of already having it, can determine the proper move to make. Players who are comfortable with this kind of thinking can quickly make mental computations that improve their decisions; over the long haul, they increase their chances of success. Equally important, they don't have to remind themselves to think this way; it is automatic.

Most of these math and computer types have done a lot of academic studying, are good at it, and for the most part, enjoy it. They bring this background to Scrabble, a game that requires a brutal study commitment, and they already know what works best for them. "Learning is fun," says David Gibson, who won the All-Stars competition in 2003, and is a professor of mathematics in Spartanburg, South Carolina. When he was learning the game, he used 17,000 flashcards to master the seven- and eight-letter words.

This ability to study requires a discipline that most parlor players don't have and can't imagine. Games are supposed to be fun, not work. At the mention of studying most parlor players balk. Top players put in tens of thou-sands of hours and keep at it. This is solitary, antisocial, drudging work. There are no rah-rah team practices or attaboys. It's just you and the words, possibly putting sports, movies, TV, and family on hold.

The top players are good anagrammers and spellers too. Some of them compete at anagrams to relax at the end of

David Gibson just after defeating Steve Tier to win the 1994
Championship in Los Angeles. The woman to his left is a
reporter, directly behind David is Lester Schonbrun, then
Martin Weisskopf, out of focus.

the tournament day. As they sit in a small group the word
in play might be REENACTS. Someone will pipe up that it
becomes CAROTENES if you add an o. Someone else will

"steal" CAROTENES by adding a D to make ANCESTORED, and on they go. These feats of anagrammatic magic are done on virtual racks in the players' heads; no pencils or paper allowed. I can't begin to do it and that's one thing that separates me and many other players from the best.

The same holds for spelling. In the everyday world I'm good, but among the letterati, I'm not. I have had to memorize my way through more words than I care to admit. Any seven- or eight-letter word that I haven't studied often turns into a phonetic misadventure. This seldom happens to top players. If they misspell a word, it's something like APOMICT, where they have forgotten the letter string, not a word like URGENCY, which I recently spelled URGENTCY (missing TURGENCY).

Many of the top players are "gamers." They played other games before Scrabble and many still do. Mike Senkiewicz, of New York, who codified tournament Scrabble for Selchow & Righter, was a top chess player. Today he earns his living at backgammon. Jerry Lerman, of San Francisco, was a chess master, played chess against Joe Edley, of Coram, New York, from 1965–68; they were bridge partners in 1969; played backgammon in 1977 and '78, Scrabble from 1978–86, and competed at Mastermind, Jotto, and assorted other games along the way. Joel Sherman, of New York; Jim Geary, of Phoenix; and Joel Wapnick, of Montreal are accomplished chess players. Ron Tiekert, of Atlanta, played bridge and backgammon.

Joel Sherman, who won the 1997 Worlds and 2002 Nationals, played chess and Scrabble with his brother Larry for many years, and competed in chess tournaments long before he got involved with organized Scrabble. Both require specialized endgame play (when there are no tiles

Joel Sherman and Matt Graham tune up for their match with
Maven for an article in the *New York Times* in 1998.

in the bag and seven or less on each rack). He and his
brother "developed a rudimentary ability to work out
endgames based on what letters were unseen, probably as
a result of our exposure to that type of anticipatory
thinking in chess."

Jerry Lerman says that once players enter the endgame,
"then Scrabble is chess." If both parties have tracked their
opponent's tiles correctly, both know what resides on the
other's rack. If the game is close, the winner will be the one
who can best think through his own potential moves, as
well as the countermoves of his opponent, to score the
maximum number of points, while he holds his opponent
to a minimum. "The player with competitive chess experience," says Lerman, "has an edge in this sort of thinking."

This desire to win has been touted by Joe Edley, the only three-time national champion, as the most important factor in becoming a premiere player. For Edley it's more than just wanting to win. It is wanting it so badly that a player will do whatever it takes in the way of study, practice, and lifestyle adjustments to make it happen. (Edley worked odd jobs that allowed him to study.) Jerry Lerman calls it "the killer instinct," and says "[it's] the idea of wanting to win so badly that you'll examine every legal method that helps." In Lerman's case, he has mastered the phony, learned to analyze his weaknesses, and developed ways to overcome disappointment.

The latter is called the ability to maintain equanimity or poise. Scrabble is not just an intellectual game; it is a psychological and emotional game. Opponents can appear to be weak or strong. The game can have its ups and downs. Tiles can turn from good to bad. Through it all, the best players know that they must keep an even emotional keel. When spirits flag, performance suffers. Overconfidence is just as deadly. All good players do things to avoid these traps.

Chris Lennon, of Oregon, feels the best way to play is with "a detached acceptance of fate." Each move is played intensely but not frantically. Losses are accepted. "No fretting, no fussing, no whining," he says. "It's amazing how, if you keep a clear head, winning chances will sometimes present themselves in what you thought was a lost cause."

In his book *The Official Scrabble Puzzle Book*, Joe Edley offers similar advice. To play to your potential, he says, it's necessary to keep track of "your own internal state." This includes tuning out distractions, forgiving yourself for mistakes, remaining emotionally neutral about the tiles, having an intense curiosity about finding the best play, and also about finding a way to win. Edley has been known to practice Tai Chi between tournament games and deep breathing while he is playing.

Everyone who plays is familiar with "the tile gods." When random tiles are drawn, even a top ten player can be beaten by an otherwise mediocre opponent because the tile gods looked favorably on one but not on the other. This type of loss is very frustrating to players at every skill level. Comments like "All my racks were drek," or "I couldn't draw a blank," are common. In theory, the more seasoned a player is, the more understanding she should be of the fickleness of the game. In fact, the more time and effort a player has invested, the more potentially upsetting it can be when the tile gods become hostile.

The stress of organized play can bring all sorts of emotional demons to the surface. Some people give up when behind, stew about poor plays or incredibly improbable draws. Others get morose in defeat, blow up at their opponents, or find it particularly difficult to lose to the opposite sex. It all boils up at one time or another and may sound like grist for a therapist's couch, which it is. One player, who prefers to go nameless, recognized that his emotions hampered his play and sought help. He worked through his anger and tendency to be overly self-critical to come out the other side a stronger competitor.

Other intangibles also play a role in being good. One is "board vision," which can seem as mundane as seeing all your options, to something intuitional, and almost mystical, when Adam Logan, of Ottawa, puts it into words. "It's an awareness (often partly unconscious)," he says, "of what is likely to happen. It involves understanding

At the Boston Area Tournament awards ceremony
in 2007, from left to right, Adam Logan, Jason Katz-Brown,
Brian Cappelletto.

which parts of the board are likely to come into play soon,
and what (if anything) one should do to encourage or dis-
courage this."

"Tells" are trickier and, according to Joe Edley, are not
used enough. The concept comes from poker, where
players watch facial tics, body language, gestures, and bet-
ting behavior looking for clues to a player's hand. The
same thing is possible in Scrabble if a player is attuned and
knows his opponent well, says Edley. Does your opponent
always slouch when she has bad tiles? Does she play
phonies quickly? Does she fidget when she has a bingo?
Top players take advantage of such tells.

Brian Cappelletto, of Chicago, agrees that "reading"
an opponent is important. Not reading his mind, but his

rack, based on the tiles he has recently played. Cappelletto's kind of "reading" involves making assumptions about the plays an opponent has made. "It works best against stronger players," says Cappelletto, "because they make fewer mistakes." If done properly, and your opponent is making the best possible plays, Cappelletto says, "you can figure out what letters are more likely to be in the bag instead of on your opponent's rack."

The best of the letterati never give up, either, which is very easy to do in a game where 100 or more points can hit the board in the blink of an eye. "My philosophy is to never give up," says Cappelletto. "If I'm down by 100 after three turns, I still have to find a way to win." Cappelletto faced one of those situations at the 1993 Western Championship in Reno, Nevada. He was behind by a bunch to Lisa Odom of Minneapolis, with one tile in the bag, the ugly AINOOOS on his rack and a chance to win if he could play a seven-letter word.

There was a one-in-eight chance to draw to the seven, because Cappelletto knew OOGONIA (the female sexual organ in some algae and fungi) and recognized that he had all the letters but the G. Because he had tile tracked, he also knew that the last G was either on Odum's rack or in the bag. So he played off his s and fished for the G. "My opponent had no idea what I was doing," he says. The G came up, "and I got to lay down OOGONIA to go out and win."

The best players have to know a lot of words, be able to find them when they have them, and know where to play them. There is more to the mechanical side of the game, though, than just knowing words, and plenty of room for mistakes. Mike Baron believes that mental errors are a major difference between the top competitors and lower-rated players. "Such errors include lapses in memory, board blindness, playing challenged phonies, allowing opponents' phonies to stand, and the poor management of time," says Baron.

Joel Wapnick, winner of the 1999 World Championship, isn't convinced that superior word knowledge is all it's cracked up to be. Wapnick votes for something he calls "playing ability," as the real difference between the high-level expert players and those who are still aspiring. He worries that too much emphasis on word study leads players to short-change the study of strategic and tactical skills that are actually more difficult to learn.

Peter Morris, of Michigan, agrees. He won the 1989 Nationals and the first World Scrabble Championship in 1991, but was known for his limited word knowledge. He says he had a strategy and executed it: he played fast, turned over a lot of tiles to get the blanks, had a good endgame, and never played defense. In retrospect Morris recognizes that tile turnover, a central principle of his game, was wrong. But he says, "While it might not have been the best strategy, I think it is important to have *a* strategy, believe it is right, and have enough confidence in it to execute it well."

Jim Kramer, of Minnesota, who won the Nationals in 2006, also pays attention to strategy and tactics. He thinks that most strategy issues have been poorly studied, and that the few rules of thumb that do exist have not been written down because there really is no Scrabble literature worthy of the name. To be good, a player must figure these things out, says Kramer, by making game-losing mistakes, asking better players, or using computer simulations.

The top players may not agree on what it takes to be

good, but it seems to be a question of emphasis. Expert players are years if not decades in the making. They are analytical types, often with a math or computer background. The game is a learned skill that requires a desire to be the best and a long-term commitment to excellence. It's a labor intensive activity, which has emotional, psychological, and mechanical components, which can all be improved. The better players are always cycling in and out of study routines, and working on their inner selves. There is no blueprint for success, and no substitute for persistence.

17

The Trademark Ball and Chain

Fettering the Organized Game

This is the point where the Scrabble story should conclude with a look at how all the hard work and dedication of the players has led to ever bigger and better things. In fact, the caliber of play has never been better. The number of player-run tournaments has never been higher. The potential for the development of the game has never been greater. This is largely due to the efforts of the letterati, not Hasbro. In fact, the letterati have no control over their destiny. Hasbro holds sway over the game and the future of the players. The company has never offered the players much in the way of rewards. There are no plans to let the top tier of players earn a living from the game. No plans for a Hasbro-backed Scrabble tour. There are no endorsement offers, no exhibitions or clinics, like in so many other sports and games. Some players are eager to do it. "I'm just saying it's time to get freakin' paid," says a frustrated

Marlon Hill. Hill thinks that if the game were promoted, the public would respond.

According to John Williams, the Executive Director of the NSA, Hasbro thinks things are just hunky-dory with Scrabble. After all, sets continue to sell. The players? Well, they have a great time playing in their self-financed tournaments, while they promote the game. Why should anything change? The players have fun. The company makes money. What could be better?

"It's really absurd," says Les Schonbrun, "that a corporation that has had literally nothing to do with creating, improving, or playing the game should wield so much control over it." He's not always pleased with his fellow players, either. "I don't know which I find more exasperating, Hasbro and its reps or my colleagues who are mesmerized by corporate power."

Everyone is not a believer. Even in the late 1970s and early 1980s, there were players who would have quit their jobs to play pro Scrabble. Peter Morris, of Michigan, would have jumped at the chance. "It would have been a niche market," he says, "not NASCAR-sized events or anything near it, but something."

Today only Joe Edley, three-time national champion, is able to say he earns a living from Scrabble. But he does this by virtue of his employment as the vice president for clubs and tournaments at the NSA. The most vocal person on the subject of professional Scrabble is Joel Sherman, the 1999 World champion and 2002 winner of the Nationals. Sherman runs the New York club and considers Scrabble his life. He is the only person who gives "Scrabble player" as his occupation. Sherman looks at chess, tennis, golf, and bowling and says, "All I ask is that

Scrabble players get equal attention, respect, and reward for the labor they put in as other sports." If one asks around, Sherman isn't the only one who would like to see professional Scrabble.

The players feel that if a Scrabble tour existed it would have no trouble finding participants. Players already go into the hole when travel and lodging expenses are added up. If there were a tour, with even modest purses, it would lure them into competing more often than they do now— while they kept their day jobs.

Jim Geary, of Phoenix, is one. "Every one of those events would generate ten times as much media exposure as well," he says. "It might cause me to spend less time playing poker and would probably get the strongest players out more too." And just maybe, the big paydays would eventually come.

This isn't happening and the players feel the root of the problem is the Scrabble trademark. If not abused, a trademark can last forever. All the holder has to do is use the mark in interstate commerce, keep others from adopting it as their own, make certain the mark doesn't become generic, and renew it every ten years. It can be lost if it is discontinued, used sporadically, becomes part of the language, or fails to designate a single source for the good in question (see Dorr and Munch, 1995). Anyone who has been around organized Scrabble for a while knows that the trademark makes its way into any serious discussion of the future of the game.

According to Jim Houle, who ran the players' organization from 1976 to '85, the trademark was part of the reason for inaugurating the organized game in the first place. Selchow & Righter wanted publicity, but it also wanted to control tournaments and clubs to make certain that the name of the game was used properly. No doubt company attorneys worried about the worst-case scenario in which the unsupervised use of the Scrabble trademark turned it into a generic term, similar to xerox and cellophane. Once that happened the game and its market share would have been up for grabs. It's about the money. For Selchow & Righter, Scrabble was the bulk of its bottom line. That is not the case for Hasbro, a multibillion-dollar concern that sells over 200 toys and games, but Scrabble is still important. In 1996 *Financial World* estimated the value of the Scrabble brand at $76 million, with 1995 sales alone at $39 million. In 2002, it was estimated that sales of Scrabble sets worldwide hit 3 million per year, in 23 different languages. A lot is at stake.

In 1971, when S&R bought the rights to Scrabble, the market was much more fragmented than today and the company found itself in an unusual position. On the one hand, it owned a very popular game that sold at the rate of a million sets per year. The game was promoted as a family activity. Yet, this simple parlor pastime could also be refined, inspire fanaticism, and be played at sublime levels by the letterati. A few unofficial tournaments had already taken place in Nevada, the New York City chess clubs, and probably other locales. The company wanted to bring this situation under control.

Concern for the mark is evident from the second issue of the *Scrabble Players Newspaper* in the fall of 1973. The company was already asking for help from its tile pushing members. "SCGP Inc. [the players' organization] would like to ask your help in protecting the trademark

Scrabble," read the first paragraph of an article imploring the letterati of the day to use the mark correctly. The *Scrabble Players Handbook*, a how-to volume, which the company published in 1974, actually had a two-page chapter devoted to the trademark and how the players should respect it, at the same time as they were told how to do the right things to protect it.

In 1973 S&R started out by licensing the mark to those who organized clubs. This didn't last long because turnout was less than expected and club directors protested the yearly licensing fee. After that, what S&R probably feared, according to Kenneth Port, who teaches intellectual property law at Marquette University Law School, was "naked licensing." The clubs were no longer formally licensed, but they were using the mark. To avoid being vulnerable in court, Selchow & Righter felt that it had to demonstrate that it controlled the use of the mark. Hence, they instituted various restrictions on the clubs, the issuance of a club director's manual, strict control of tournaments, and all the trappings that have been put in place over the years.

By and large this strategy has been successful. To this day most tournament flyers produced by the players contain a trademark symbol, ®, after the name Scrabble. Even online, some players add the ® to communications about the game. A few report "Scrabble sightings," when the game appears in TV shows, ads, books, or movies, perhaps unwittingly giving a heads-up to Hasbro's legal department, which is always on the look-out for unauthorized uses. Many players feel they are doing their duty, that they are saving the game from malevolent outside forces.

Most of the player complaints over the years have had their roots in the trademark. Whether it's the restrictive publishing policy, the prohibition on outside tournament sponsors, or the claim that only those sanctioned by the NSA can run Scrabble clubs and hold tournaments, it all comes back to the trademark. The holder has always claimed it had the right, and maybe the duty, to keep Scrabble on a short leash, to protect its mark. The impression left with the letterati was that everyone was supposed to genuflect to the mark.

Organized Scrabble is in the position it is, at least in part, because of the changes in trademark law that have occurred over the past fifty years. These changes have encouraged mark holders to claim that their trademarks are not just production designations that distinguish their widgets from someone else's, but actual property. This, in turn, has led to ever-greater claims for protection.

Robert Denicola, who teaches intellectual property law at the University of Nebraska Law School, says that it's common practice for mark holders to assert more rights than they have. It doesn't cost much, typically the postage on a "cease and desist" order. "The recipient usually doesn't have enough at stake to justify litigation," says Denicola. "The practical effect of a trademark can thus be much greater than the actual legal limits of the protection," he says.

In the case of Scrabble, more than money could be at stake. People have talked and written about perceived injustices in the Scrabble world, most notably Al Weissman in the mid 1980s, but no one has come forward to challenge the status quo. And for good reason. If a malcontent got on the wrong side of the trademark holder, she just might find herself excommunicated from the NSA, which would mean no more tournament Scrabble for her. Paranoia? "Some players would rather lose their jobs than not be able to play in tournaments," says Les Schonbrun.

18

A Chilling Effect

Squelching How-To Books

The number of independent Scrabble how-to books published in North America the past thirty years can be counted on one hand; parlor players might conclude that no one has anything to say. Not so! People write about Scrabble, but the books usually don't get published.

It all started in 1972, when Mark Landsberg, a California player, penned a manuscript he called "Championship Scrabble Strategy." Landsberg knew Scrabble was a trademarked game, so he sent a copy of his manuscript to Selchow & Righter, who owned the game back then, and requested permission to use "Scrabble" in the title.

At the time, Selchow & Righter was hatching a plan to develop tournament and club Scrabble. The company also wanted to publish a players' handbook, according to court documents, but had no manuscript. When he saw Landsberg's book, Lee Tiffany, who ran the players' organization, asked Scrabble expert Mike Senkiewicz to evaluate it. Senkiewicz says today that he didn't think it was very good, although court documents show that he gave it glowing praise in 1972.

Selchow & Righter negotiated with Landsberg for several months. Finally Landsberg concluded they were leading him on; he broke off talks and asked the company to return all copies of his work. But Senkiewicz kept a copy. Then he wrote the *Scrabble Players Handbook*, which Selchow & Righter rushed into print in 1974. Landsberg sued for copyright infringement; in January 1979, before the case went to trial, Lee Tiffany settled for $11,000. But S&R and Crown Publishers soldiered on. The case dragged out for eight years. What began as a copyright infringement case ended as a breach of contract case (Landsberg had been led to believe that Selchow & Righter wanted to publish his book). It cost S&R somewhere between $600,000 and $800,000. (Read more about the case in the Appendix.)

A few players knew Landsberg had won, and that Selchow & Righter had tried to take advantage of him. The case made the relationship between the company and the players clear: they were adversaries. It made no difference that the players were the company's goodwill ambassadors.

The seeds of suspicion were reinforced by another publishing incident. This time Senkiewicz was the wronged party. He regularly received royalties from the *Handbook* published by S&R, but sometime in the mid 1970s, when Crown took over the title, the royalties stopped. Senkiewicz knew a high-powered lawyer who sent the company a letter of complaint. He had to negotiate a lesser royalty, but he got something. "It cost me money," says Senkiewicz, but it was cheaper than going to court.

About the same time Senkiewicz proposed the idea for an official Scrabble dictionary, including the basic approach of scouring five collegiate dictionaries for words and combining the results. He and some friends even did preliminary work on it. When he pitched the idea to the company, S&R offered a meager royalty, about a tenth of what Senkiewicz thought the project was worth. He refused. Then the company took the idea to G. and C. Merriam, who published the *Official Scrabble Players Dictionary* in 1978. "There wasn't much I could do about it," says Senkiewicz.

Selchow & Righter didn't seem to have much respect for the rights of the players, or for the dictionary publishers whose volumes it culled for the *Official Scrabble Dictionary* words, but it insisted that its rights be protected. In 1976 Mason/Charter Publishers of New York was about to publish *The Scrabble Book* by Derryn Hinch. It was already a Book-of-the-Month-Club (BOMC) selection, which guaranteed large sales.

S&R claimed that the book infringed both its trademark and copyright, particularly the book jacket, which contained the word Scrabble, spelled out with tiles. The company also argued that sections of the book were copied directly from the *Scrabble Players Newspaper*. S&R's lawyers considered it a prima facie trademark violation and wanted a preliminary injunction to stop publication. The judge didn't see it that way. "This failure [to show irreparable harm] precludes issuance of preliminary injunctive relief," he wrote. The company also argued that sales of the *Handbook* would suffer if *The Scrabble Book* were published. Again, the judge disagreed. This is an important but seemingly forgotten precedent in the world of Scrabble publishing. It says, contrary to what the manufacturers have always claimed, that a writer can publish a Scrabble how-to book without kowtowing to the trademark holder. It doesn't say, though, that the trademark holder won't sue.

Ask Joel Wapnick. He won the North American Scrabble Championship in 1983. In 1985 he wanted to publish *The Champion's Strategy for Winning at Scrabble Brand Crossword Game* through Stein and Day Publishers of Bay Shore, New York. Again S&R sought an injunction to prohibit publication. The publisher cited the Book-of-the-Month-Club decision and indicated it was going ahead.

Soon they were negotiating. Wapnick recalls that he was told by Stein and Day "that either there is an agreement or there is no book." This was because Stein and Day was in financial difficulties of its own and couldn't afford a protracted court battle. So Wapnick went along with an arrangement to give S&R 25% of his royalties, not including the $6000 advance. Just after the book was published Stein and Day folded. "S&R got nothing," says Wapnick, "because the book went out of print before I could earn money beyond my advance."

An interesting aside to the case occurred at the 1985 Scrabble Symposium. Jim Neuberger, a New York player and lawyer, asked Richard Selchow why S&R was suing Joel Wapnick. Selchow insisted "we are not suing Joel Wapnick," not knowing that Neuberger had copies of the court documents. The incident piqued Neuberger's interest in trademark law. He discovered through his research that S&R had overstepped the law when it went after Stein and

Day. "They had no right to suppress a book about Scrabble," says Neuberger, "as long as the publisher made it clear who owned the trademark."

One Scrabble player who did publish was Al Weissman of Westerly, Rhode Island. Weissman had been a chess player at the Fleahouse in the 1960s and '70s and had fond boyhood memories of reading the chess masters. When he married an accomplished Scrabble player and switched games, he was shocked to find that there was no comparable Scrabble literature. With his wife Donna he set out to right that omission.

From 1980 through 1986 they published *Letters for Expert Game Players*, which missed only four monthly issues over that six-year period. It was written for the top players, people who wanted more analysis than the official newsletter offered. A group of twenty or so experts submitted solutions to problems laid out in the *Letters*. There were never more than fifty or sixty subscribers, but it was photocopied and passed around.

Weissman thought s&r's publishing policy stood in the way of the development of the game. This resulted in his *Letters* taking on an editorial tone in March 1983 when he reproduced an article from the *New York Times* that explained how the game Monopoly had lost its trademark, because in the minds of consumers the name of the game was not synonymous with the name of the manufacturer, Parker Brothers. Weissman seemed to imply that Scrabble was no more synonymous with s&r than Monopoly had been with Parker Brothers. Did he have insurrection on his mind?

Weissman felt the intellectual content of the game was not owned by the company, but belonged to the players.

He resented the company's claim of control over publishing. "People should be free to write about it." Weissman felt that the game needed a generic name, one that could be used by the players instead of Scrabble, without fear of legal repercussions. This solution came naturally to Weissman because he was a pharmacologist familiar with the generic versus trade distinctions common in the drug industry.

In his April 1985 issue, he said, "I broached a sensitive topic in the last *Letters* [a generic name], and perhaps even a dangerous one." He went on to say that he wanted to open up the *Letters* to "criticism of the Scrabble scene." "Many of us," he wrote, "if not all, know the fervor such discussions arouse in casual conversation among experienced players." Weissman thought the development of expert players had been thwarted by the company and its players group. He argued that the protection of commercial rights was fine, but that the suppression of free speech through trademark law was not.

Weissman wrote what many top players were thinking. In his May 1985 *Letters*, he received kudos from players like Joel Wapnick, Jim Pate, Bob Schoenman, and Jim Neuberger, while some supporters asked for anonymity, apparently out of fear of reprisal.

Weissman suggested the generic name of QAID. He envisioned a QAID society to deal with rules, event scheduling, ratings, and the dictionary, rather than having it done by "corporate hacks." He wanted to see books and magazines devoted to QAID, as there were in chess. Mike Baron referred to him as "the Johnny Appleseed of Scrabble." Other subscribers worried that Weissman was courting disaster. "They will sue you and you should

Jim Neuberger at the 1983 Nationals in Chicago with his annotator.

count on it," wrote one anonymous player.

Weissman felt uneasy enough to discuss his situation with a lawyer. He says he was never threatened, "but I definitely felt their hot breath on my neck." The editorials cooled. In the May 1986 issue, the Weissmans announced they were bowing out of the *Letters*. They said that they were tired, wanted more personal time, and felt they had accomplished most of what they had set out to do. It wasn't long before they stopped playing tournaments. The protest was over.

In 1987 S&R received royalties when Michael Lawrence and John Ozag published *The Ultimate Guide to Winning Scrabble Brand Crossword Game*. It's the only independently written how-to that has ever passed muster with the trademark holders. Why? Lawrence was a well-known writer with a dozen bridge books under his belt. The book was aimed at beginners, the hoards of parlor players who were already S&R customers. It had the potential for mass-market appeal.

Lawrence was a writer who knew very little about Scrabble, but wanted to learn. Ozag was a player who couldn't write, but knew the game. Lawrence recalls that the company received some portion of the advance. "There was a lot of formalized bullshit," he says, but they worked it out without animosity. "They were sort of assholes about it, but I had an attorney who wrote some nice letters."

The Lawrence and Ozag book proved to be the exception. In the late 1980s, for example, Bob Watson of Minnesota, who won the Nationals in 1988, was at the Western Championship in Reno. His roommate was Jim Kramer, another top Minnesota player. Kramer had been playing well, but on the third day of the event fell ill with food poisoning, was unable to get out of bed, and had to forfeit a number of games. Watson noticed that his fellow players "seemed to me to welcome Kramer's illness as a boon for their own chances to win." The idea for *The Scrabble Murders* was born.

Coleco, the new owner of the trademark, liked the idea, says Watson, quite possibly because it was having financial problems. Watson wrote four chapters and signed up with agent Jonathon Lazear. Lazear lined up Delacorte Press, which offered Watson a two-book deal and a $30,000 advance. Coleco went bankrupt and Milton Bradley (an arm of Hasbro) bought Scrabble. The deal was quickly bogged down in Milton Bradley's licensing division. As Watson remembers it, "The company began making unreasonable demands on the publisher, and the whole deal descended into a gridlock that lasted over two years before falling apart." Milton Bradley wanted a fixed percentage of the retail price of every book published, while Delacorte was only willing to pay a fixed percentage of the profits, since many books would be given away in promotions and most would be sold at various discounted wholesale prices. By then Watson had written the entire novel and had a good start on the second. In the end there was no deal and he never saw a penny for his efforts.

This was not an aberration. Rita Norr submitted a proposal to do a how-to book. "We spent a year in negotiation with their lawyers," says Norr, who was the 1987 National champion. She wanted to be able to use the word Scrabble on the cover. Not a chance. There were arguments about the writing that would appear on the book boxes and whether Milton Bradley had the right to inspect the publisher's warehouses.

Elizabeth Frost Knappman was Norr's agent. "It took a year out of my life," she says, "and it was a nightmare." In retrospect she feels that part of the problem was that the lawyers for Milton Bradley didn't understand publishing, but also that working in such a large bureaucracy it was difficult to get anything done. The negotiations collapsed.

In 1988 Mike Baron and Jerry Guin self-published *The Wordbook*, which deconstructed the *Official Scrabble Players Dictionary* into usable word lists and provided suggestions for studying them. During the writing, Guin was so concerned about trademark suits, says Baron, that they never used the word Scrabble and even avoided the word "tiles," substituting "letters" instead. The book was an instant hit with the letterati, but sales were limited because of the small number of serious players. In 1991 Baron tried to get the official Scrabble imprimatur, which could make the book an Avon mass market publication and a desirable item in bookstores. The unfortunate Knappman simultaneously represented Baron and Rita Knorr. Knappman would later write to the trademark holder, "These agreements have floundered over pettyfogging details that were irrelevant to the protection of your trademark." Baron persisted, privately publishing until 2007, when Sterling Publishing picked up his book. Because Sterling published Hasbro puzzle books, it managed to get Baron the Scrabble imprimatur he had sought for sixteen years. (Sterling is wholly owned by Barnes & Noble.)

These and stories like them have percolated through the Scrabble subculture. So players have been afraid to write. In the early 1990s Nick Ballard had the book bug. He loved to write, was deeply interested in Scrabble theory, and already published *Medleys* newsletter. "I would have enjoyed writing something highly theoretical, but I just didn't want to deal with the red tape," or share the proceeds. Bob Felt acknowledged that the Scrabble book scene was impoverished, but says, "I have no intention of writing a book without prior assurance that Hasbro won't stonewall publication."

Brian Cappelletto observed that "I'd love to sit down and write a book or a series of books on how to play the game, but I am definitely discouraged by the process that I've heard so much about." He thinks there are two options: jump through the hoops of the company's legal department and probably not get published, or self-publish, since no commercial publisher is eager to do battle with Hasbro. His advice: "Hope the judge interprets the law your way."

Not long ago Jim Geary approached Joe Edley at the National Scrabble Association with a book idea. Edley told him that first he had to get a publisher, and then Hasbro's legal department would say yes or no to the idea. Geary had the material ready to go, but this gave him pause. He had a lawyer friend who offered to do pro bono battle with Hasbro. Geary decided it was all too much trouble.

Since 1988 Joe Edley has been in charge of tournaments and clubs for the National Scrabble Association. He is the only person who has Hasbro's approval to write how-to books. He has put out two in the past ten years. Hasbro has done a good job of scaring the bejeezus out of everyone else.

The real losers are the public and the organized game. Books about Scrabble would expose more people to the organized game, increase the number of club and tournament players, and probably sell more Scrabble sets. Imagine a shelf of them at your local bookstore. Most of the letterati see that as a win/win scenario, but apparently not Hasbro.

Its latest attempt to control the written word was only partially successful. In the summer of 2003, the company applied to the Patent and Trademark Office to extend its mark to all written matter having to do with Scrabble (dictionaries, reference books, activity books, workbooks, story books, crossword puzzle books, instruction manuals, and books). The request was denied. (A reconsidered brief for all written matter other than books was successful.) Thus exposing what many already knew, that it has no control over books, even if it does own the Scrabble trademark. Players may one day look back on this denial as a bright day for the organized game.

At the same time as books have received short shrift from the game's owners, so have Scrabble computing projects. In retrospect everyone understands that the use of computers in Scrabble revolutionized the game, yet these advances might have come much sooner if S&R had not stood in the way of Stanley Rabinowitz. As early as 1978 Rabinowitz, who works at Digital Equipment Corporation in Massachusetts, developed a Scrabble playing program with co-worker Richard Lary. It was called PQS-Scrabble and incorporated many of the features that would take another fifteen years to appear in other programs. Rabinowitz tried to convince the company to let him give it away in the Digital electronic library. No luck. The program did not go beyond Digital's Massachusetts facility.

The programs that had an impact on the organized game—Tyler from Alan Frank, Jim Homan's Crosswise, and Brian Sheppard's Maven—came along a decade later. They had to tread lightly. What the program developers did, according to Homan, was engage in anti-marketing. They hoped this would give them a low profile and allow them to fly under the trademark holders' legal radar. It also limited sales. They didn't name their programs Scrabble, advertise them as Scrabble, or claim they played Scrabble. They sold by word of mouth.

In 1996, Hasbro came to serious computer Scrabble, largely by accident, when it acquired Maven, from Brian

Sheppard. (Hasbro only learned of the program by chance.) Sheppard was thrilled to give it up after some thirteen years of development. Hasbro expurgated the dictionary and cut some features, but it was a far better program than anything it had previously sold.

That was not the end of the computing story. In the late '90s, probably in response to Maven, Homan decided to improve Crosswise. According to John Hart, a California player, who beta tested the program, it was good. Then there were legal rumblings from Hasbro. Homan threw in the towel and even shut down his decade-old business, which specialized in after-market Scrabble paraphernalia. E-mails to him go unanswered.

Two Scrabble enthusiasts from Calcutta had a go at bringing their favorite game online, creating a knockoff version called Scrabulous in 2006, which is free for users and generates its revenue from advertising. Within a year, they had 600,000 registered users but it was the social networking website Facebook that really kicked it into high gear. As of January 2008, the Scrabulous application on Facebook had 2.3 million active users. And Hasbro noticed. But rather than take over Scrabulous and its legions of enthusiastic users, according to *Fortune*, they are trying to shut it down. Still the creators, Jayant and Rajat Agarwalla, are hopeful that "some kind of deal" will be reached.

19

Growing the Game

Squelching Outside Funding

Scrabble is an infectious game. Once it gets in a person's blood it often takes over the host. Family, friends, other pastimes can get put on hold or discarded. Early on some players recognized this. They reasoned that if they could feel this way about the game, so could others. They came to believe that the game had an unrecognized potential, that it could catch on in a big way if properly promoted. Yet, at every turn they met with roadblocks from S&R. One of the first to meet with disappointment was Milt Wertheimer.

Wertheimer came on the Scrabble stage in the 1970s. "I tried to commercialize the game," he says, "because I thought it would generate a tremendous amount of interest if done correctly." Wertheimer put on the Nathan's Famous Tournaments in New York's Times Square; they were held once a year for five years in the late 1970s and attracted from fifty to eighty players. Wertheimer dreamed of events with real prize money and outside sponsors—book publishers and soft-drink makers, among others. He talked to Jim Houle who ran Scrabble Crossword Game Players. "I was stopped dead in my tracks by Selchow & Righter, which was only interested in protecting its trademark."

Houle says he couldn't support Wertheimer's approach. "He wanted to get people involved who we couldn't control." Houle recalls that there had already been assaults on the Scrabble trademark and that other well-known products had lost their trademarks, so he was particularly sensitive to the problem.

One of Houle's assignments at S&R was to assist the legal department in protecting the mark. He sorted through Scrabble-related magazine and newspaper articles forwarded to the company by a clipping service. He set aside those he felt used the trademark improperly or without authorization. "When we found them," he says, "the legal department would send out cease and desist letters." Adds Houle, "I probably knew more about this than anybody. I protected the trademark and I knew its history."

He certainly protected it from Wertheimer, who started clubs, organized tournaments, and played seriously for a decade, all in the hope that one day he would see the game that he loved take the world by storm. "This was one of the major disappointments of my life. I loved the game and I think it could have exploded, but instead of support, all they did was restrict me." Over the years he attended the Nationals, but didn't play—instead he sat at the first table in the first division, where the top two players were duking it out, while he annotated their games for publication in the newsletter.

Jeff Kastner shared the dream with Wertheimer. Kastner was a nineteen-year-old chess master when he discovered serious Scrabble at the Fleahouse in 1969. To publicize the game in the late 1970s, while he was the manager of the Manhattan Chess Club, he organized a non-credit course at NYU. For his trouble, "after my third week I received a letter from Houle saying that I was in violation of the Scrabble trademark." Houle threatened to sue, Kastner ceased and desisted and says, "That incident left a very bad taste in my mouth for organized Scrabble that I have to this day."

Gary Brown remembers those cease and desist orders too. He was active in organized Scrabble from 1973 to 1990. Brown had learned to play while stationed in Great Britain in the early 1970s. When he returned to New York in 1973, he immediately dove into the Manhattan chess clubs. At the same time he wrote Scrabble strategy articles for *Games Magazine* in the UK. "I got a letter signed by Lee Tiffany telling me that I was infringing on their trademark," says Brown.

In the early 1980s, says Houle, both Selchow & Righter and Seagram were represented by J. Walter Thompson, the ad agency. The idea of sponsorship was floated by the agency, says Houle. "I said no and I brought it to the attention of management and they said the same thing." S&R was a small company of perhaps 140 employees, according to Houle. To them Scrabble was a family game and they wanted to keep it that way. "It could have gotten out of control," he says.

Charles Goldstein remembers the Seagram's rumor. In retrospect, he says, "We could have been on the map if that [sponsorship] had happened." Goldstein says that many of the letterati of the time hoped that Scrabble would eventually be able to support professional players. Kastner has similar recollections. "I and most of the other top players were hoping to see Scrabble become a big money game," he says.

For Selchow & Righter it was always about PR and control, while for the players it was about advancing the organized game. What confuses the matter for the letterati is that there never has been a clear statement from the owners to that effect. John Williams has periodically engaged in a charade in which he laments that the company "doesn't get tournament Scrabble," implying that when it does the game will flourish. While the letterati wait, some kick around ways to jumpstart the game.

Bob Lipton feels that Scrabble needs a Bobby Fischer. He has lobbied Williams and various Hasbro execs to include a flyer in every game box, which would contain the picture of a top player, along with a list of his or her Scrabble accomplishments. "Hasbro does not want Scrabble to be a big-time sport, or if it does, it doesn't have the slightest clue how to make it so," says a frustrated Lipton. There are no pictures and there are no stars.

Another road to growth could be through outside sponsorship of tournaments, something much feared by little S&R, but what about today's multibillion-dollar trademark holder? IBM, for example, has sponsored chess tournaments and there are countless other examples. Many players think it could work.

In an online discussion, Audrey Tumbarello, of New York, suggested creating an audience for Scrabble by showcasing the game on public access TV. Rita Norr replied, "I hope you pack your *OSPD*, Franklin, and a

Scrabble set when you leave for jail." Susi Tiekert wrote, "They [Hasbro] do what they want, when they want, how they want. Give it up. You're knocking your heads against a brick wall . . . the company owns us."

The corporate view of all this is much different. Hasbro doesn't stand in the way of tournament Scrabble, according to Williams. To the contrary, it's supportive. It funds the NSA, the Scrabble in the Schools Program, the Nationals, and the World Scrabble Championship, where the Nationals alone cost around $300,000 (recently Hasbro bowed out of the Worlds). "They feel the publicity from the clubs and tournaments sells games," says Williams.

He provided a rare glimpse into the corporate thinking on the Nationals in the March 2003 *Scrabble News*. "The company wants," wrote Williams, "the National Scrabble Championship to take place in a Top 40 market that has a daily newspaper, several network affiliates, and a major league sports team." Outside money is another matter. Williams says when it comes to Scrabble, the company really has nothing to sell to an outside sponsor.

Williams has even said that Hasbro is quite happy with selling two million Scrabble sets a year and wouldn't want to see a spike in sales due to some large promotional effort. "Remember," says Williams, "the company is thrilled with the way Scrabble is selling, and they manufacture over 200 different products. It's not as if the executives we deal with can devote a huge amount of time to thinking about a product that from their point of view is doing just fine."

This gets to the crux of the problem, from the players' perspective. Hasbro is doing fine. But it costs players more to travel to tournaments and compete than they can hope to recoup in prize money. "If you go to a lot of events, and you don't win any money," says Brian Cappelletto, "it gets very expensive."

Not all competitive Scrabble players are unhappy. Not even all the top players are disgruntled. Many have successful careers that they would never give up for Scrabble. Others are content to play "for fun." Some wait for the big paydays that probably will never come.

Company execs are anonymous and remote. They don't communicate with the players. The corporate go-between is John Williams, head of the NSA. When asked if there is a long-term vision for the letterati and the game, his response was revealing. "There is none," he said, "as I've tried to emphasize, the company looks at this year to year. Everyone assumes the scene will go on as it is, but it has not been addressed."

In 1987, the National Scrabble Association created a Scrabble Advisory Board, to give the players some say in the direction of the game. But Paul Avrin, a longtime New York player, sees it as an exercise in frustration. "All the Board can do is make recommendations to management," he says. "But they don't talk to us," says Avrin.

To be fair, the players have had some say about the rules of the game, the word source, and the ratings. Many are pleased with the present situation. They are thankful to the various trademark holders who have owned the game over the years. They point to the fact that there was no tournament Scrabble prior to the involvement of Selchow & Righter and suspect that there still wouldn't be, without the company's backing.

At various times there has been talk of an independent

players' organization. One that would not merely do the bidding of the trademark holder. Marlon Hill, a Baltimore player, wrote on CGP, the Scrabble electronic listserv, "What kind of players' organization has zero accountability to the players?" He said the NSA was ineffectual and "prevented the growth of the game." In Hill's opinion, it was time for a change. "If you don't represent my interests," said Hill, who wants to see big money tournaments, "get out of my way."

He got a response from Joe Edley, vice president for the NSA, who pointed to all the good things the organization was doing that would lead to what Hill wanted—in maybe ten years. (Edley told me, "I have no idea when it will happen. Could be ten years, could be twenty, thirty, or never.") He told Hill to get involved in a positive way. Edley proposed a Scrabble video to give players a higher profile and raise public awareness of the game. But then he lamented the lack of NSA money for such a project and asked, "Anybody want to volunteer their time and effort?" Continuing his tone deafness, he also suggested that Hill volunteer for the Scrabble in the Schools Program and that players might want to donate money to the NSA so that one-on-one annotated matches could be held. It's hard to believe, but the only player to earn a living from the game fielded a complaint about the lack of money in tournament Scrabble by asking the letterati for donations. Only in Scrabble.

When an angry Hill would have none of it, Edley tried again. This time he was less conciliatory, telling Hill that his whole approach could blow up in his face. Hill's public ardor cooled a bit, and, in good bureaucratic fashion, Edley suggested that existing NSA player committees could address his concerns if they were put in writing. The 700 or so observers to this exchange were left to make of it what they would. The underlying message seemed to be clear: if a player criticizes the structure of the NSA, he could expect push back. The letterati received it. Posts on the topic dried up overnight.

It's a bit odd, and certainly a source of some of the players' irritation, that a PR/marketing firm, largely funded by Hasbro, but also by player dues, runs the players' organization. It didn't side with Hill; it threatened him. Maybe the people who think about Scrabble for Hasbro don't care one way or the other. What can a few players do? And the joke is on the letterati. They are an unpaid staff of goodwill ambassadors who pay the company to play, since they must be NSA members to enter tournaments. Then, they crisscross the continent at their own expense showcasing the game. What a concept. It's easy to see why the company would be upset if someone questioned it.

2 0

Don't Ask What Hasbro Can Do For You . . .

Working on the PR Plantation

One might expect that because of this history of publishing, sponsorship, and promotional rebuffs, that the players would have a pretty low opinion of Hasbro, but this isn't universally true. Some of the longtime letterati harbor grudges, but many others either don't know about the past, choose to ignore it, or think that Hasbro owns Scrabble and can do as it pleases. Those who are disgruntled should just shut up and play the game.

A segment of the players go out of their way to promote Scrabble. It's easy to see why. Even if they are unhappy with the status quo, they remain addicted to playing. How could they restrain their enthusiasm for something they love? Even if a player doesn't applaud the company, she cheers for the game. All one needs to do is follow the posts on the Scrabble listservs to get a sense for this. The letterati alert fellow players to every media mention of the game. They set their VCRs to catch a three-minute interview with the latest national champ. They are ga-ga for the game.

The company has the letterati right where it wants them and takes advantage of the situation at every turn. To paraphrase President Kennedy, don't ask what Hasbro can do for you, but what you can do for Hasbro. And the players do many things. To start with, they run the more than 200 North American clubs. This means there are meeting notices on public bulletin boards, in newspapers, at libraries, game shops, and on club websites, year in and year out. These notices help keep Scrabble in the public consciousness. No one is paid for this. Clubs also put on tournaments. To organize them requires a large commitment of time. Flyers must go out, the site must be acquired, and someone must see to the logistics. In my five years of experience with the Denver event, these efforts have generated two major newspaper articles and one TV story. No one is paid for this, either.

The letterati want coverage. Everyone hopes that it will bring in fresh blood. The Boulder club has been happy to cooperate with newspapers in the writing of three Scrabble articles. Multiply this coverage over some 200 clubs and that's a lot of free publicity. A good chunk of John Williams' corporate report card is based on the number of articles that were published in the previous twelve months.

There's more. Club members participate in local events to recruit members. We had a booth at the Rocky Mountain Book Fair. We showed the flag, played all comers, and hoped a few would become members. Players do this throughout North America in one way or another. Again, no one is paid.

The trademark holder also partners with Proliteracy Worldwide. The company gets its name associated with a worthy cause and participants make donations to PW. Quoting the NSA website, "This ongoing program results in positive exposure for the Scrabble brand in key markets across the country." Members of a local Scrabble club play matches with the public, it's a nice fundraiser for PW and most players enjoy doing it. But on the players' end, no one gets paid.

The latest scheme is the Scrabble in the Schools Program. Jim Houle says that as far back as the late 1970s, Selchow & Righter wanted to get into America's schools to plant the Scrabble seed and sell games. When the company got down to the specifics, it discovered that it didn't have the manpower.

The Educational Task Force at the NSA makes it work. It coordinates the activities of the NSA Volunteer Corps, which is made up of letterati who go into America's middle schools to help teachers set up Scrabble programs and run tournaments. On the NSA side it was run by the marketing and projects director, Yvonne Gillespie, who did get paid.

A headline in the October 2002 newsletter said, "We Need U." The faithful were told that they could help develop the next generation of Scrabble players. What could the letterati do? A lot, as it turns out: visit a school classroom; phone a teacher or administrator; meet with an educator; meet with or start a school club; mention the Volunteer Corps at a club meeting; start a club at a local school or library; conduct educator workshops; write an article for a newspaper; present School Scrabble materials at PTA; recruit Volunteer Corps members; volunteer at a local school Scrabble Championship; or work with a newspaper to promote a School Scrabble event.

The schools are given a break on the cost of the games, while the students have fun and benefit from the spelling, vocabulary, and math skills that are honed by competing. Hasbro sells games both to the schools and probably to the parents of the kids who participate in the program. It also establishes a beachhead among the next generation of players. Pretty slick.

It's nice that kids play Scrabble but let's not forget what motivates the company. Hasbro is trying to sell games as it associates itself with worthwhile educational goals. That's good PR and business too. One has to wonder, if the players stopped volunteering for the program, just how committed would Hasbro be?

But that's not all the players do. The letterati buy logo embossed gewgaws of various kinds that they sport in public, further keeping the spotlight on the game. Sweat-shirts, T-shirts, tote bags, hats, pens, coffee mugs, and dozens of other things all bear the Scrabble logo. Not that long ago there wasn't much of this gear around. One player commented on a Scrabble listserv that "I feel obligated to promote the game and recruit whenever possible." Shortly thereafter the "Word Gear" catalog appeared.

The clubs are de facto PR offices scattered across the land. It's a testimony to the infectiousness of the game that many of the players have this loyalty to the brand. Many of the players are glad to do it. They want to share their fervor for a pastime they love. They don't see their volunteer efforts as contributing to the corporate bottom line, but rather to the growth of the organized game. At least most of them don't.

Lester Schonbrun (R) tells filmmaker Eric Chaikin how it is, while waiting for the award ceremony to begin at the 2002 Nationals in San Diego. Eric was at the tournament filming the documentary *Word Wars*.

Paul Sidorsky, a member of the Calgary, Alberta, club, doesn't like it. Sidorsky thinks the clubs are small and tournaments limited because people have to pay the NSA to start clubs and run tournaments, which means that only "diehard fans" get involved. "They should be paying us to promote their product," he says. The one-sidedness of the relationship bothers him, too. "I try not to think about it," says Sidorsky.

The same goes for Lester Schonbrun, of Oakland. He gets particularly resentful of the trademark holder during the biennial Nationals "when it gets free publicity from the tournament, extracts in the neighborhood of $60,000 in entry fees from the players (and possibly gets kickbacks from the hotel), and still acts as if it is doing us a great favor," says Schonbrun. This was in evidence at the 2002 San Diego Nationals when the 689 attendees were asked to hold their applause until all the NSA staff had been introduced. The letterati were supposed to recognize these people for doing their jobs. There was even the implication that these employees had made great sacrifices for the game. No one thought to mention that players coming from the east coast might have spent $1000 for their week of Scrabble. It was very much an atmosphere of "look at all we do for you." Not, "thanks for all you do for Hasbro."

The competitive Scrabble world continues to tread water as the letterati promote the game. This situation frustrates the top players, but they don't see an alternative. "We aren't going to repeal the golden rule," said the late Bob Felt, "and Hasbro has the gold, and rules."

21

Arrested Development

Resentment Among the Letterati

The National Scrabble Association often deflects criticism of the Scrabble status quo with the assertion that the game is still in its infancy. To paraphrase, "Be patient, good things will happen. Remember, chess has been around for hundreds of years. One day Scrabble will come into its own." Scrabble's predicament is not the result of infancy alone. The trademark holders' policies have arrested the development of the game. This has ensured an indefinite infant-like status.

There are consequences. The players are not allowed to see if they could earn a living from the game. Because of this the trappings of professionalism have never developed. The lack of outside sponsors, how-to books, and professional players shapes the public's perception of the game. The game is seen as just a fun diversion. When some players take it seriously, they appear a little loony.

The lack of Scrabble how-to books is one of the things that affects the public perception of the game. Certainly, there's a need for such books, but there is more to it than that. Due to the shortage of books, the myth that Scrabble is just about vocabulary and spelling lives on. It implies there is nothing to learn. If libraries and bookstores contained shelves of Scrabble tomes, a different message would be sent: "There's a corpus of knowledge here that the best players have mastered. If you want to be good, you will have to master it too."

Scrabble's arrested development also affects the people who play in clubs and tournaments. Many don't feel the effort involved in striving for excellence is worth it. It has no monetary payoff and it takes too much time. At some point in the journey from novice to expert, they stop trying, even though they still enjoy the game. Fair enough. But the decision to coast has ramifications. The coaster begins to lose more. His national ranking slides. Because he is competitive, he resents this.

The skill differential between the top players and everyone else, which exists in any competitive endeavor, sometimes fuels this resentment. It can result in an anti-elitism that is not seen in sports and games that are allowed to flower, where the distinction between the professional and the amateur is clear and well understood. In Scrabble, the best players are not universally viewed as models to be emulated. Some lower-level players even claim to view them with pity or scorn. Anyone who has been around the game for a while has heard comments like "Those guys don't have lives," and "You'd be good too, if that's all you did."

Compare that to golf, tennis, or other sports. Middle-level players are in awe of their champions. They flock to tournaments and gather in sports bars to get a glimpse of the game at its best. No one would suggest that Tiger Woods or Venus Williams don't have lives. Nor would they argue that Woods and Williams spend too much time practicing. Not so in Scrabble. The unspoken message is Scrabble is just a game.

Bob Lipton puts the blame for this at the feet of John Williams, the executive director of the National Scrabble Association. "We're caught in a web of John Williams' making," says Lipton. "He insists on building Scrabble from the bottom up." In practice this means the *Scrabble News* sometimes runs features on lower-rated players, lauds their accomplishments, and in the process lessens the space given to the top letterati, unlike what is done in other sports and games. "In every endeavor but Scrabble," says Lipton, "excellence is admired."

The *Scrabble News* reflects this. It never takes on an advocacy role for the players, or criticizes the status quo. It presents the company's position, sells the company's products, and talks up Scrabble as a fun hobby. It doesn't prod the membership toward a professional future or even entertain the possibility that someday one might exist. The obvious conclusion is that Hasbro isn't interested in more expansive possibilities for the game.

This all helps to feed what Brian Cappelletto, winner of the 2001 Worlds, sees as resentment of the top players. He's been told, for instance, "You're a nice guy for a 2000 rated player." This bothers him because he thinks most top players are nice guys, who live normal lives outside of Scrabble, and as a whole are no more eccentric than any other group of people. He hates it, for example, when the grooming, physical, or employment foibles of a few players are seized upon by journalists to make their Scrabble stories more colorful, rather than highlighting the normalcy of most players. He feels it alienates the top players from everyone else, making them look like oddities, "and who wants that," says Cappelletto.

He also thinks this resentment is fueled by the delusion on the part of some players who believe they could be the best if they just put in the time. He feels this is nonsense. These players are essentially saying that their lives are too rich and fulfilling to spend endless hours poring over word lists. Hence, comments like "the top players don't have lives," which is really a justification for a lack of diligence, in Cappelletto's view. Can anyone imagine some duffer telling Tiger Woods that he's a nice guy, considering he's the best player in the world? Only in Scrabble.

The way tournament prize money is allocated can also contribute to resentment. The letterati finance their purses through entry fees. In many events the largest prizes go to the top players, who are partially subsidized by the players in the lower divisions. The expert players usually feel that excellence should be rewarded, while many of the lesser players resent contributing to that reward. This inequity, as the lower-division players would characterize it, helps to stir the resentment pot. Cappelletto says the resentment is not what it was a decade ago, but it's still there. In the end he thinks it comes back to legitimacy. "If we made seven figures being top players, the pursuit would be validated."

Jerry Lerman, another top player, agrees that Scrabble masters don't get much respect, but says that from a purely economic perspective he can understand that. He says that it's easy to question the economic wisdom of committing large chunks of time to Scrabble. On top of that, the best players usually win about the same size purses as middle-level players, he says, which rewards mediocrity. "Until lower-rated players see the top players make money worth their while, they'll have justification to question the top players, rather than be in awe of them," he says.

Lerman thinks there are things that would help top players get more respect. In bridge, the best players are hired as partners by lower-ranked players, who want to learn the game. Top bridge players also write books, something that is all but impossible in Scrabble. Top chess players get even more respect than bridge players, says Lerman. Grandmasters and International Masters are revered. "Their idiosyncracies are seen as endearing, and aren't subject to ridicule." Chess masters write books, give exhibitions, and teach. None of those things are available to the letterati, says Lerman.

Ironically, there is anti-elitism in Scrabble. Because the game has been infantalized, many players are not ready to applaud an all out quest for excellence. Most people don't want to talk about this, but recently Cappelletto raised it on the CGP electronic listserv. "I think nearly every idea that gets brought up seems to be tested for elitism (meaning bad) or egalitarianism (meaning good). What's with that," he wrote. "I definitely feel there is a prevailing form of political correctness in this game, and the biggest cardinal sin is showing any signs of elitism."

Some elements of the tournament structure have a psychological leveling effect. The top players still play in the same tournaments, and usually in the same room, as everyone else, even though the best players are light-years ahead of the pack in skills and commitment. But because there is no money in the game, that's the way it has to be.

This anti-elitism reflects another issue that separates the letterati into two camps. Is Scrabble just a game that should be played for fun, or is it something more, a serious undertaking? Those near the top have long concluded that Scrabble is more than just a game. But for many of those further down in the ranks, this is far from clear. This popped up in another post that also appeared on CGP. "Is tournament play for fun and enjoyment by as many people as possible," wrote this disgruntled player, "or is it for the Scrabble snobs who look down their noses at lower-division players?"

Reading between the lines of some of the comments that I've heard over the years, there's the suggestion that those who excel have no right to be that good. There are even attempts to minimize their Scrabble accomplishments by tearing them down as people. For instance, "Player X is good, but you wouldn't want to have a conversation with him."

One of the reasons for it, I think, is that players are recruited from around America's kitchen tables, where they rule their respective roosts. None of them have ever seen the game played at a high level nor have they had the opportunity to read about its finer points. Many probably feel that it's a bit unfair when they learn that their Sunday afternoon pastime is more than just a game to the letterati.

Because the game has been infantalized, the culture which surrounds it is immature too. It's still acceptable to express anti-elite feelings without fear of censure. It's still weird to commit one's life to the game. It's still chic among some players to say, "I don't study." But, this isn't the only game to reach such a crossroads. Some sixty years ago Ping-Pong players faced a similar situation. They were under the control of a game maker. They had divisions within their ranks. Perhaps something could be learned from their experience.

22

The Ping-Pong Precedent

Breaking With Parker Brothers

Is there a way out from under the Hasbro umbrella? The case of Ping-Pong offers some tantalizing parallels. Ping-Pong was also trademarked. It was controlled by a game maker—Parker Brothers. The company put on tournaments in the 1920s and 1930s that were sanctioned by the American Ping-Pong Association (APPA), which was an arm of Parker Brothers, much like Scrabble Crossword Game Players was an arm of Selchow & Righter and the National Scrabble Association is controlled by Hasbro. If the Ping-Pong players wanted to compete in APPA events, they had to use Parker Brothers equipment.

By the beginning of the 20th century, much like Scrabble, the right to sell Ping-Pong was held by two companies. In North America it was Parker Brothers, while in the remainder of the world the British firm of J. Jacques &

Sons held sway, according to Tim Boggan, who has written a history of table tennis.

In 1926 the European players broke with Jacques. They formed the Table Tennis Association. In the United States, there were pockets of players all over the country who played with local rules, makeshift equipment, and lots of enthusiasm. Parker Brothers wanted to standardize play and in the process sell equipment. It owned a chain of fifty Spalding Sporting Goods stores that sponsored local Ping-Pong tournaments. To aid its efforts at standardization and market dominance the company formed the American Ping-Pong Association (APPA). The company held posh events at swank hotels for those who agreed to use Parker Brothers equipment. The players resented this control. They wanted to use their own rackets, for example, and also wanted recognition from the fledgling International Table Tennis Federation (ITTF), formed after the European players freed themselves from Jacques. But the ITTF would not recognize the APPA as long as it had commercial ties to Parker Brothers.

In 1931 the Metropolitan Ping-Pong Association of New York voted to leave the New York Ping-Pong Association (NYPPA) and become the New York Table Tennis Association (NYTTA). The top player of the day, Marcus Schussheim, joined the rebels. Soon a competition for members between the new NYTTA and the Parker Brothers–backed APPA was in full swing.

The break-away group put on its own Nationals in 1932 at Bambergers, a down-scale New York department store. The same year the APPA held its Nationals at the posh Waldorf-Astoria Hotel. Parker Brothers depicted Ping-Pong as highbrow. It recruited movie stars, including

Harold Lloyd, Fay Wray, and Ginger Rogers, into its western branch of the APPA. At the same time, table tennis was portrayed as the poor man's game and given ethnic connotations. Schussheim was the product of a tenement upbringing and owned a messenger service.

By 1933 a number of local Ping-Pong groups had shifted allegiance to the rebels. To avoid a complete schism, the players tried to persuade Parker Brothers to allow them to use their own equipment in tournaments, but the company wouldn't budge. No doubt it assumed the players would never give up the well-funded events that it sponsored for an independent but impoverished existence. It was wrong. In 1934 the players formed the United States Table Tennis Association (USTTA) in Philadelphia. The USTTA represented over 1500 players from organizations in New Jersey, Illinois, and Philadelphia. They never looked back.

The most obvious lesson for Scrabble is that once the players changed the name of the game from Ping-Pong to table tennis they were able to walk away from the Ping-Pong trademark. "They couldn't continue to call it Ping-Pong," says Boggan, who writes for *USA Table Tennis Magazine*, "so they called it table tennis, which is more generic." This may explain why Al Weissman tried to stir up interest in a generic name for Scrabble. He was aware of the Ping-Pong saga and may have hoped Scrabble's troubles could be resolved in the same way. Probably Selchow & Righter's lawyers knew what happened to Ping-Pong and did not look kindly on Weissman. This view is seconded by Glynn Lunney, Jr., who teaches intellectual property law at Tulane University Law School. "Certainly S&R would have been concerned about such a usage," says Lunney, "and might even have threatened legal action (though the legal basis for such action would not be clear)."

Independence from corporate control has not been a panacea for table tennis. According to Boggan, table tennis in Europe and Asia has gone on to great popularity, with the top players able to earn a good living, but that hasn't happened in North America, where the game has never caught on. "You can't make a living just by playing," says Boggan. Some players survive by coaching, giving exhibitions, writing books, and selling equipment. Much like Scrabble, says Boggan, "most players go into the financial hole so that they can play."

They do have their own players' organization. It makes the rules, sanctions tournaments, and tries to make the game, which has been an Olympic event since 1988, grow. It has a bimonthly magazine, as well as sponsors such as Bank of America, Texaco, and various equipment makers, who contribute to prize funds. The USTTA works for the good of the game and not a multinational corporation, and the players are able to preserve the hope that one day the North American game will flower.

The question is: could the letterati break away from Hasbro, or at least have a greater degree of autonomy than they have now?

23

Scrabble and the Law

Academe Weighs In

Over the past quarter century, trademark law has played an important role in the development of organized Scrabble. What follows is not legal advice, but rather a preliminary exploration of some of these trademark issues.

The owners of Scrabble have never hesitated to assert their right to control the game. According to some experts in the field of intellectual property law, the companies may have pushed the envelope, with the knowledge that the players haven't had enough at stake to oppose them.

According to Glynn Lunney, who teaches intellectual property law at Tulane University Law School, the Ping-Pong players were on to something back in the 1930s. "This would probably work today," says Lunney, in a discussion of the Scrabble situation. The letterati could just walk away from the trademark, declare they were playing a different game, and start over. Trademark protections have expanded since 1948 when Scrabble was registered, but the company has to live with the protections that were granted at the time of registration. "There are no retroactive expansions," says Lunney.

It could be premature to do any celebrating, according to Marquette University Professor Kenneth Port. "If we were living in 1933, I'd tell you to rock and roll," he says, "but intellectual property rights have changed a lot since then." Port thinks that if secessionists used Scrabble boards in their tournaments, even if they claimed that they were not playing Scrabble, that Hasbro would view it as a violation of trade dress. On top of that, says Port, because tournaments would be involved, the company might claim a commercial use of its product, which is trademark infringement.

One way around this might be to modify the game; use the generic elements (the alphabet, a blank board, the making of words), but change the premium squares, the point values of the tiles, and so on. "The question in the end," he says, "is how much did you take? In trademark law the answer will depend on whether you created a likelihood of confusion. Would most average users of board games look at your game and assume it came from or was sponsored by Hasbro?"

Even without seceding, the letterati may have more options than they think. A publishing lore has grown up within the Scrabble community, encouraged by the owners, which contends that no one can publish anything related to the game without the trademark holders' blessing.

Hasbro has been at its best when would-be writers have accepted its hegemony and sought its imprimatur. The

writers and their agents have been worn down in an endless negotiation process. Most legal run-ins, though, have
been of the cease and desist variety, where Selchow &
Righter scared off the author, or, as in the case of Joel
Wapnick's book, bullied him into accepting a profit-
sharing arrangement.

Then there's the 1976 Book-of-the-Month-Club case
(the Derryn Hinch book), where BOMC went to court and
won. The case is virtually unknown among the letterati. It
suggests that the protections claimed for the mark are not
as absolute as the holder would have the letterati believe.

A doctrine called "nominative use" has grown up to
protect writers and publishers. A trademark used in the
title of a book, even if it is held by someone else, is considered lawful if it describes what is in the book. This is
called "a non-trademark use of a trademark." It's not used
as a trademark for the book, the publisher, or the writer.

Nor is its use intended to dupe the consumer into
buying the book because it has the trademark on it. It's not
a deceptive or confusing use, because if done properly, no
one will think that the book was published by or for the
mark holder.

The owners do have the right "to prevent commercial
uses of the mark that cause consumer confusion," says
Mark Lemley, who teaches intellectual property law at UC
Berkeley's Boalt Hall. Nominative uses are not considered
commercial uses. If someone is writing a book on the history of competitive Scrabble, "you can call it *The History
of Scrabble* without infringing the trademark, and without
a license from the owners," says Lemley. "A Scrabble
strategy book should be okay too," he says, "as long as
the author makes very clear (on the cover and elsewhere)

that it is unauthorized." (Since the 2004 expansion of the mark, this may not be true for strategy books.)

Hasbro's control of tournaments may also be a stretch of its rights, according to Lemley. "It's not at all clear to me that the trademark owners actually have the right to control tournaments," he says. "What they can probably do is prevent any use that suggests or implies to consumers that it [a tournament] is 'authorized' or 'official.'"

Robert Denicola, who teaches intellectual property law at Nebraska College of Law, says that because the trademark holder is already associated with tournaments, "it would be hard to run a competition that used the trademark in a prominent way without running a fairly big risk of liability." If it were called something like "The Crossword Tournament Using the Scrabble Game (not affiliated with Hasbro)" someone "would have a good argument," says Denicola, "that they haven't infringed either the game mark or the tournament mark because the use doesn't create any likelihood of confusion." That is, the man on the street would not think that the tournament was sponsored by Hasbro.

The clubs may be a different story, but even there it's not black and white. In 1973 Selchow & Righter licensed the clubs, with yearly renewals, and weekly remittances. This was short-lived, but may have been an attempt to create something akin to franchises. In the case of a franchise, the franchiser controls the quality of the service or product produced by the franchisee. The clubs don't actually make Scrabble sets, says Lunney, so "whether the clubs are enough like a franchise that it would make sense for the law to require the trademark holder to supervise the clubs in order to maintain the Scrabble trademark is less clear."

If they didn't control the clubs, though, others might start them and uncontrolled use of the mark could follow. This is called "naked licensing." So what the owners have done is understandable. "If a trademark owner fails to police its mark and allows others to use it freely," says Lunney, "there's a risk that the mark will become generic."

Even that is iffy. Denicola says that trademark owners often cite "a duty" to police their marks as a justification for threatening users. "In fact," says Denicola, "the duty is quite minimal," basically to stop confusing uses that might lead a consumer to think that these uses are sponsored by the trademark holder. Denicola thinks the validity of the Scrabble mark "would not have been threatened if the company had made no effort to control its use on books about the game or on tournaments in which the game is used."

Why did they do it? Denicola offers two possibilities. First, never underestimate corporate culture. "Procedures and policies sometimes accumulate in corporate counsel offices," he says, "and then take on a life of their own." On the other hand, says Denicola, "there is often an advantage in extending the significance of a mark into new markets." When it comes to tournaments and books, if the trademark holder can get people to associate the mark with them, and not just the board game, "the company is in a position to capture some of the potential value of those markets if they ever become lucrative."

There is another possibility, says Marquette's Port. The company shares the mark with Mattel/Spear, which sells Scrabble sets outside of North America. Port has represented similarly bifurcated trademarks and says they are always weaker than one that is solely owned. "This must have Hasbro worried," he says, because of what is known as the "single source" test in trademark law.

If party A goes to court to invalidate party B's mark, party B must show that consumers believe there is only one source for their product. The determination is made by surveying the public. The respondents have to think that only one company makes the product. The consumer is not supposed to be "confused" about this. When two companies share a mark, confusion is more likely. That's why Port is puzzled by the joint website access that Mattel and Hasbro once shared and their former co-sponsorship of the World Scrabble Championship. Both muddy the "single source" waters.

One way to foster the illusion of a single source, says Port, is to control the trademark in as many venues as possible. In the case of Scrabble this could mean sanctioning clubs and tournaments, not allowing outside sponsorship of events, obstructing how-to book publication, and generally appearing to be in control.

In 1971, Selchow & Righter was in a weaker position than Hasbro is today, says Port, because the trademark was trifurcated, because T. R. Urban and Company held the rights to Scrabble in Australia. Then, in the late 1970s, the AntiMonopoly case (in which Parker Brothers objected to a game called AntiMonopoly) was wending its way though the courts. One of the questions the case turned on was whether the public thought of Monopoly as a board game or as a source of a product. The conclusion was "board game," a descriptive and generic use of the mark. It was ruled invalid.

The same question could have been asked of Scrabble. To blunt this line of attack, Selchow & Righter produced a glut of products under the Scrabble brand name: Scrabble Dominos in 1978, Scrabble Lexor Computer Word Game in 1981, Scrabble Crossword Cubes, Duplicate Scrabble, Scrabble Ipswitch and Scrabble Upper Hand, all in 1984. As far as the company was concerned Scrabble didn't merely denote a board game (generic use), it referred to a brand name and a whole line of products. Bring on the surveys. Today the above products are long gone, but others have taken their place. To reflect this "brand," rather than "game" view of the world, Hasbro wants Scrabble referred to as "the Scrabble Brand Game," or "the Scrabble Brand Crossword Game," not just Scrabble.

The game is in a legal limbo quite different from the view held by the various mark holders. The situation is more amorphous than the letterati have been led to believe. This does not necessarily change real world outcomes. Take the publication of books, says Lunney. Anyone who ended up in court would probably win, but court costs would typically exceed the royalties from sales. So no one publishes.

It could be argued that we are back where we started. The legal deck is stacked against the letterati at the same time as they probably have far more rights than they could have imagined. Still, the exercise says a lot about the trademark holders.

There has never been a special relationship between the players and the companies. There have been no attempts to encourage how-to book writers, entrepreneurial tournament organizers, or players who wanted to be professionals. When it comes to making money from the game, the players have always been stalemated. For the companies, it has just been business.

24

The Future

Options for Growth

Some would argue that the future of organized Scrabble looks quite promising. They see the glass as half full. They look back on three decades of complete obscurity and see that the game has come a long way: tournament Scrabble is occasionally on TV and there have been several Scrabble documentaries. There are more tournaments and good players than ever before. There is a growing school Scrabble program. *Word Freak*, by Stefan Fatsis, was a best-selling book. And public awareness of serious Scrabble has never been higher. That's all true, but as someone who has observed the scene for a decade, and researched its history, I remain skeptical. For me, the glass is half empty.

The trademark holders have made business decisions in the hopes of selling more games, which have in many instances stood in the way of serious Scrabble. It has been the players that have actually provided the impetus to grow the game. Recently, Hasbro announced that it would no longer sponsor the World Scrabble Championship (because their market is North America). It has also made clear that it will take legal action against the World English Language Scrabble Players Association if it tries to function in North America. And in 2004 it tried to extend its copyright to all written materials relating to Scrabble. These are not the actions of a company interested in the long-term development of the game. The top players won't be giving up their day jobs any time soon.

So it should come as no surprise that there is no plan for the future of organized Scrabble, according to John Williams, who heads up the National Scrabble Association. It's all year-to-year. Even though in many ways Williams is the NSA, this lack of a plan extends to what will happen when he retires, which might not be that far off. "I kind of envision a scene like the one in *The Wizard of Oz*, where the house has landed on the Wicked Witch and everyone is dancing around," he says. What about the game? The NSA is just an account at Williams and Company. According to Williams, Hasbro can do as it pleases with the NSA, should he retire. He could be replaced, the account could be snapped up by another agency, or who knows what.

That's not the kind of answer a serious player wants to hear. Yet, it's part and parcel of Scrabble's dilemma. Decisions made by faceless, nameless, corporate suits have far-reaching implications for the letterati, but appear to be based on criteria that are unrelated to growing the game.

Steve Polatnick, of Florida, thinks secession from the NSA might be the answer, but in the same breath worries

From left to right, John Williams, David Wiegand and his children, and Panupol Sujjayakorn at the award ceremony for the 2005 Nationals in Reno. (Note: Williams is holding an ESPN microphone.)

that it could also set the game back, since the number of tournament players is small and cash to support a rival organization is limited. "If we had hundreds of thousands of members then we could kiss the NSA off," says the Florida attorney, "even if there might be some legal issues."

The letterati have proved quite docile. Most non-elite players don't care about these issues and those at the top have dollar signs not revolution on their minds. In August 2003, ESPN, the sports channel, covered the final game of the All-Stars Scrabble Tournament, an "organized-for-TV" event in which David Gibson of South Carolina pocketed $50,000. Many letterati saw this as Scrabble's big break, or at least they hoped it was. Recently John Williams has said that ESPN's ardor has cooled. If the players don't try to influence what happens, no one else will.

In 2007, inspired by the World Poker Tour, Steve Pellinen, of Minnesota, proposed the North American Scrabble Tour. The basic concept is to have a series of one-day local tournaments that will send winning players and a portion of their entry fees to a final event at the end of the year. Pellinen deserves an A for effort. As usual a player comes up with the idea.

A different approach comes out of Southeast Asia and possibly the remainder of the world. It's too early to tell what might come of it, but a handful of tournaments have sprung up in Malaysia, Singapore, and Thailand that offer anywhere from a few thousand to $15,000 to the winners. They have sponsors and apparently can operate with more latitude than Scrabblers in North America or England because Western law is not yet firmly entrenched there. Might the future of the game lie offshore? Perhaps.

At the 2003 Worlds, which took place in Malaysia, an organizational meeting was held for the World English-Language Scrabble Players Association (WESPA) and there were promises of a $100,000 prize for a tournament to be held in the near future. Invitees included the heads of national Scrabble organizations from eighteen countries (the NSA declined to send a representative). Allan Simmons, Chairman of the Association of British Scrabble Players, was ready to chair the meeting, when word arrived that if the group tried to function in North America, Hasbro would take legal action. Undeterred, the meeting went forward, the group formed, and Malaysian Scrabblers offered to house its headquarters.

So there is a desire to unite English-speaking players.

Whether this is analogous to the struggles that wrested Ping-Pong from the control of Jacques and Parker Brothers seventy-five years ago remains to be seen. It does have parallels. In the UK the players run their own association, even if it is tied to Spear and Company, which holds the rights to Scrabble outside of North America.

Many players feel there is something refreshing about the world's most skilled practitioners of the game attempting to take control of their destiny. There is little question that if serious Scrabble proved to be financially viable, Hasbro would be there to reap the low-hanging fruit. There has been almost no mention of WESPA on CGP, the Scrabble electronic listserv. No doubt the letterati who are aware of it do not want to offend their sometimes patron. Whether North American players will participate in WESPA is still an open question.

Some have suggested that the letterati are a sleeping giant; that they could strike out on their own if they wanted to. What if, they say, 1000 players girded for battle, anted up $500 each, recruited pro-bono legal muscle from their ranks, and managed to get the 200 or so Scrabble clubs in North America to work as their PR arm?

What if?

Afterword

In 2007 the National Scrabble Association announced that Hasbro would allow outside sponsorship of tournaments. Nothing happened. No guidelines. No encouragement. No tournaments.

Then, from September 28–30, Matt Hopkins, a long-time Philadelphia player and tournament director, put on his Baltimore event, with backing from local financial institutions.

The secret: Hopkins married school Scrabble to tournament Scrabble. He had already brought Scrabble to the inner city of Philadelphia. To do it in Baltimore, and obtain tournament sponsorship, he proposed that a portion of tournament entry fees go to the school program. Hasbro liked it.

Hopkins says Hasbro gets out of the way as long as the trademark is protected and the Scrabble logo is prominently displayed. "We mention their name at every opportunity," he says.

It wasn't major sponsorship—the top prize was $5000—but it was a beginning. Hopkins would like to see it done the same way in other cities.

The trick was making everyone look good. The sponsors and Hasbro are able to associate themselves with bringing Scrabble to underachieving, inner city schools. The local politicians like it too.

"Hasbro will also benefit," says Hopkins, "because this will expand the future market for the game." The kids will become lifelong players.

A player's idea. But a special player. Hopkins is a paid Hasbro consultant. Could any player do what he did? If so, does it have to be done the way he did it? Time will tell.

The Landsberg Case

Mark Landsberg, a California player, submitted a Scrabble how-to manuscript to Selchow & Righter in 1972. He wanted permission to use Scrabble in the title. He felt the company led him on and then published its own book (the *Scrabble Players Handbook*) in 1974, using many of the concepts from his manuscript. Landsberg sued for copyright infringement in a California district court.

The judge heard the testimony of Lee Tiffany, head of SCGP, the company-owned players' organization. Tiffany said the company wanted to publish Landsberg's manuscript. Tiffany's assistant, Drue Conklin, testified that she had never read the manuscript before editing the *Handbook*. Mike Senkiewicz testified that he was not influenced by the manuscript (but while he wrote the *Handbook*, he had a copy of it in his apartment). Senkiewicz's admission that he had lifted whole sections from books on chess strategy when writing the *Handbook* probably didn't enhance his credibility, either, even though Scrabble players who know him say that he knew far more than Landsberg and didn't need to steal from him. A report from Senkiewicz to the company was introduced at the trial; in it Senkiewicz said that the Landsberg manuscript was "excellent and on the whole meritorious."

The judge concluded that while the *Scrabble Players Handbook* wasn't copied from the Landsberg manuscript, it did paraphrase it "and was used as a model by Selchow & Righter." He ruled it was a copyright violation that deprived Landsberg's work "of a viable commercial market," and added that Selchow & Righter's infringement "was knowing, intentional, deliberate, malicious, and oppressive." He further accused Selchow & Righter of litigation that was "unnecessary, unreasonable, vexatious, oppressive, obdurate, and in bad faith. . . ." With damages, court costs, attorney's fees, and profits from the *Handbook*, the judgment reached about $440,000.

To this day Senkiewicz can't believe the company lost the case and claims that Landsberg's attorneys wanted to settle for court costs at the time, but that Selchow & Righter's attorneys were so confident of victory that they rejected the offer. David Prinz, the company's expert witness (and later winner of the 1978 North American Invitational), was also shocked to hear Landsberg had won. He thought the manuscript was a joke. "It was like some patzer claiming that Kasparoff had stolen his ideas," says Prinz. He spent many hours comparing the *Handbook* to the manuscript and was convinced that in the eyes of an expert player there were more differences than similarities.

Prinz never testified in the first trial, or in the second one, when both sides appealed. At the second trial, the court ruled that while similarities existed between the manuscript and the *Handbook*, such similarities would be expected in a nonfiction work where two authors wrote about the same set of facts. The judges threw out the original copyright infringement verdict, but said there could be grounds for a breach of contract action and remanded the case back to the district court.

The district court found a breach of contract because Selchow & Righter had implied that it would publish the Landsberg manuscript but had no intention of doing so. The court upheld the $440,000 judgment, tacked on $100,000 in punitive damages, along with 10% interest on the original judgment, since the case had dragged on for five years, and threw in the profits that had been earned by the *Handbook* in the interim, which brought the award to about a million dollars. This was appealed again and Landsberg was upheld, but the judgment was revised downward to somewhere in the neighborhood of $600,000 to $800,000. Various players, though, say that over the years Landsberg has cited the figure of $750,000.

Glossary

Most of the terms in the glossary are from a list compiled by Jim Pate, who is a member of the Birmingham, Alabama, club. They can be found at http://www.geocities. com/pate.geo/newterms.html. I have supplemented the Pate list with material from a list that appeared anonymously on CGP, the electronic Scrabble listserv, and added a few items that I felt needed inclusion.

ALPHAGRAM—The alphabetical sequencing of letters, which comprise a word. Ex. ACCEKPUS is the alphagram of CUPCAKES. (Coined by Joe Edley and Jim Homan)

AMBILEXTROUS—Having the ability to switch between two lexicons in competitive Scrabble. (Coined by Lawren Freebody)

AMIWORD—A word (usually short) that looks like the misspelling of a common word. Ex. FIRN, BIBB, CONN, LONGE. Named after Ami Tzubery, a young Israeli player, initially a poor speller, who realized early on that others in the club "expected" him to misspell words and were challenging him almost automatically. He began to study the dictionary and compiled a secret list of apparent misspellings to lure challenges from those who didn't study. (Coined by Sam Orbaum)

ANAHOOK—A letter that can be added to a group of letters that can then be anagrammed into a word. Ex. The letter "s" is an anahook for PETIOLA—the letters can be arranged to make SPOLIATE. (Coined by Nick Ballard, popularized by John Chew)

ANAMONIC—A word or phrase that is a mnemonic device to indicate which letters can be added to a set of letters to make valid words. (Coined by Bob Lipton, popularized by Nick Ballard and John Chew)

BINGLET—A non-bingo play of fifty points or more.

BACK HOOK—A single letter which can be added to the end of a word on the board. Ex. FOLIOS plus an E becomes FOLIOSE.

BINGO (noun)—A play using all seven tiles on the rack simultaneously that scores a bonus of fifty points in addition to the regular score of the word or words played. (First print usage by Mike Senkiewicz)

BINGO (verb)—To play all seven tiles from the rack on a single play. (First print usage by John Turner)

BLOWOUT—A one-sided game in which one player gets all the good tiles and wins easily.

BRAIL—To feel for the smooth surfaces of the blank when drawing tiles. Only possible with wooden tiles.

BRILLIANCY—An ingenious move which floors your opponent and dazzles onlookers.

CATAGRAM—A word that has no anagram. (Coined by Dan Pratt)

CLOSED BOARD—A board situation that offers no openings for bingos.

COFFEEHOUSING—Talking to your opponent (whistling, humming, etc.) with a view to distracting him from the game. Frowned upon in club and tournament play.

DINGLE—Relating to, designating, or being a special challenge rule wherein on the second and subsequent occasions of a player making an unsuccessful challenge that player is penalized by missing a turn.

DOUBLE-DOUBLE—A word that spans two double word squares and earns four times its initial point value.

DOUBLE CHALLENGE—A rule of play whereby the challenger forfeits a turn if his or her challenge is incorrect.

DUMPING—Making a low-scoring move which rids one's rack of awkward letters.

ENDGAME—The last few moves of the game. They are important if the game is close, because positional finesse can determine the outcome.

EXCHANGING—The act of forgoing a turn to discard bad tiles.

EXPERT PLAYER—Someone with a rating over 1700. This would put him or her among the top 250 players in North America.

FAST BAGGING—Drawing tiles very quickly after making a play. This is usually done when a player is unsure of the word he has played, or is certain that it is a phony. The intent is to draw so rapidly that his opponent will not have the opportunity to get a good look at the suspect word before the act of tile drawing ends the turn and makes a challenge impossible.

FISHING—Playing off one or two tiles in the hope of picking up a specific tile or tiles to form a bingo.

FRONT HOOK—A letter that can be added to the front of a word on the board. Ex. VARIOLE becomes OVARIOLE with the addition of an "o."

HOT SPOT—A square or area of the board that offers the opportunity for a high scoring play.

HUMONGO—A bingo that scores over 100 points, particularly one that is played over two triple-word squares simultaneously. (Coined by Jim Pate)

LEAVE—The tiles left on a player's rack after a move is made. The leave can be good or bad.

MNEMONIC—A device intended to assist the memory. Ex. Each unique letter in the phrase "Makes Excellent Herb Tea Giving Food a Powerful Buzz," combines with the stem TISANE to form 69 seven-letter words.

MOXBIB—A phony word that is so outrageous that it is likely to draw a challenge. (Coined by Joel Wapnick, popularized by Peter Morris)

NEGAMONIC—A word or phrase that is a mnemonic device to indicate which letters can not be added to a set of letters to make valid words. (Coined by Jere Mead)

NINE-TIMER—A move that covers two triple-word bonus squares, scoring nine-times the initial value of the word played.

NONGO—1. A seven-tile play which will not fit on the board because either the seven-letter word will not legally hook to another word or because the board does not contain one or more other letters in the proper position for a valid play to be made. 2. A group of seven letters that in itself does not produce a valid word but that can produce valid words with the addition of certain other letters. (Coined by Jim Pate)

OPEN BOARD—A board with openings for bingos and other high scoring plays.

OSPD—The abbreviation for the *Official Scrabble Players Dictionary*. First published in 1978, the OSPD is in its fourth edition and is primarily used in North America by parlor players.

OSW—The abbreviation for *Official Scrabble Words*, a list of allowable words derived from the British *Chambers Dictionary*. Until it was recently combined with the OSPD to form the SOWPODS list, it was the word source used in the UK.

OVERDRAW—Taking too many tiles from the bag.

OVERLAP—A move in which one word either partially or completely overlaps another vertically or horizontally.

PARLOR PLAYER—A person who plays Scrabble at home, but not at clubs or in tournaments. Often referred to as a "kitchen table player."

PALMING—The unethical act of retaining tiles in the palm of the hand when drawing new letters or slipping undesirable ones back into the bag.

PASSING—Skipping a turn by neither making a move nor exchanging tiles.

POWER TILES—The J, Q, X, Z, four Ss, and the two blank tiles.

PREMIUM SQUARE—Any square on the board that doubles or triples the value of a letter or a word.

PROTILE—A type of tile having larger than standard letters and made typically of plastic with a smooth face so that blank tiles cannot be distinguished by feel from tiles containing letters. (Coined by Bob Schoenman)

Q-STICK—When a player realizes his opponent has the Q near the end of the game and blocks all possible places to play it and then slowly plays out. Or, if there are no places to play it initially, slowly plays out his tiles for maxiumum points, all the time making sure that he does not inadvertently create a Q opening.

RACK MANAGEMENT—Making moves that leave a nice balance of vowels and consonants on one's rack.

SETUP—A move that sets up a hook for a specific letter or word.

SCRABBATICAL—1. A sabbatical in which a person schedules travel so that a maximum number of Scrabble sessions can be played by visiting clubs, tournaments, and individuals along the way. 2. A planned, extended absence from Scrabble play, particularly in clubs and tournaments. (Coined by Stu Goldman)

SINGLE CHALLENGE—A rule of play whereby a challenger does not lose a turn if the challenged word is acceptable.

SNAPBACK—1. A retort of more than 50 points to a first

turn "JQXZ" five-letter play by the opponent consisting of extending the word to the triple-word square, particularly during the first few turns of a game (also referred to as a "comebacker"). Ex. COT-QUEAN, BAN-JOIST, VER-JUICE. 2. Any other single-turn extension from an initial play that extends to a triple-word square including an eight-letter bingo from or to the letter on the starred center square. (Coined by Mohan Chunkath)

SOWPODS—A combination of British and North American word sources for use in some international Scrabble tournaments. The word comes from a combination of the letters in OSPD, an acronym for the *Official Scrabble Players Dictionary* (the former North American word source) and the letters in OSW, an acronym for *Official Scrabble Words* (the former British word source). (Coined by Joe Edley)

THREE-PERCENTER—Any tile with a frequency of 3 or greater (ADEGILNORSTU). They are the 1- and 2-point letters and account for 75% of all tiles. A three-percenter bingo is one which contains such letters, with the additional requirement that the frequency with which any such letter may be repeated in the word is as follows: A-3, D-1, E-4, G-1, I-3, L-1, N-2, O-2, R-2, S-2, T-2, U-1. (With the exception of the S, this represents the number of possible triads of each letter in a full bag.) Ex. ANESTRI and ADAGIOS are three-percenter bingos while DUODENA and UNUSUAL are not. (Coined by Mike Baron)

TILE-TRACKING—The practice of using a tracking grid or letter frequency list, typically printed on a score sheet, to keep track of the letters that have been played during a game.

UNRECOGNITIS—A temporary inability to recognize a common word, which sometimes results in an embarrassing challenge. Ex. Thinking that APPLY is the comparative of APPLE or that DOOR is a noun meaning "a person who does something." (Coined by Stu Goldman)

VOWELITIS—The continuous drawing of an unwieldy number of vowels.

Bibliography

Anspach, Ralph, *The Billion Dollar Monopoly Swindle*, American Printing, San Francisco, California, 1998.

Anspach, Ralph, "10 Years in Court with Anti-Monopoly: The High Cost of Justice," *Antitrust Law & Economic Review*, vol. 16, No. 3, 91–109, 1984.

Anspach, Ralph, "10 Years in Court with Anti-Monopoly: The High Cost of Justice (II)," *Antitrust Law & Economic Review*, vol. 16, No. 4, 15–30, 1984.

Anspach, Ralph, "10 Years in Court with Anti-Monopoly: The High Cost of Justice (III)," *Antitrust Law & Economic Review*, vol. 17, No. 1, 11–30, 1985.

Anti-Monopoly, Inc. v. General Mills Fun Group et al., U.S. Court of Appeals, Ninth Circuit, Dec. 20, 1979.

Anti-Monopoly, Inc. v. Hasbro Inc., Toys 'R' Us, Inc. and K Mart Corporation, 94 Civ. 2120 (LMM), U.S. District Court for the Southern District of New York,

958 F. Supp. 895, 1997.

Ballard, Nick, *Anamonics #1–2100*, Games Medleys, San Francisco, California, 1994.

Ballard, Nick, *Medleys*, January, 1991–February, 1993, Seattle, Washington.

Baron, Mike and Gere Guin, *The WordBook*, Wordbooks and Listmats, Corrales, New Mexico, 1988.

Baron, Mike, *Scrabble Wordbook*, Sterling Publishing, New York, 2007.

Boggan, Tim, *History of U.S. Table Tennis*, U.S. Table Tennis Association, 2000.

Brown, Ralph, "Advertising and the Public Interest: Legal Protection of Trade Symbols," *Yale Law Journal*, vol. 108, 1619–1661, 1999. Originally published in 1948.

Dagitz, Mark, "Trademark Parodies and Free Speech: An Expansion of Parodists First Amendment Rights in L. L. Bean, Inc. v Drake Publishers, Inc.," *Iowa Law Review*, vol. 73, 961–973, 1988.

Denicola, Robert, "Trademarks as Speech: Constitutional Implications of the Emerging Rationales for the Protection of Trade Symbols," *Wisconsin Law Review*, 158–207, 1982.

Dorr, Robert and Christopher Munch, *Protecting Trade Secrets, Patents, Copyrights and Trademarks* (2nd Ed), John Wiley and Sons, Inc., 1995.

Dreyfuss, Rochelle, "Expressive Genericity: Trademarks as Language in the Pepsi Generation," *Notre Dame Law Review*, vol. 65, 397–424, 1990.

Edley, Joe, *The Official Scrabble Puzzle Book*, Pocket Books, New York, 1997.

Fatis, Stefan, *Word Freak*, Houghton-Mifflin, Boston-New York, 2001.

Folsom, Ralph and Larry Teply, "Trademarked Generic Words," *Yale Law Journal*, vol. 89, 1323–1333, 1980.

Frank, Alan, *Scrabble Rules* (5th Ed), Boston, Massachusetts, 1991, self published.

Goldman, Stu, *Confessions of a Compulsive Tile Pusher*, Stu Goldman Publications, San Francisco, California, 1992.

Heban, Linda, "Trademark Genericism after Anti-Monopoly," *Toledo Law Review*," vol. 15, 1601–1630, 1984.

Hinch, Derryn, *The Scrabble Book*, Mason/Charter Publishers Inc., New York, New York, 1976.

Horwitz, Ethan and Benjamin Levi, "Fifty Years of the Lanham Act: A Retrospective of Section 43(a)," *Fordham Intellectual Property, Media And Entertainment Law Journal*, vol. 7, 59–72, 1996.

Kimura, Diane, *Sex and Cognition*, MIT Press, Cambridge, Massachusetts, 1999.

Landsberg v. Scrabble Crossword Game Players, Inc. et al., 212 USPQ, 159–165, 1980.

Landsberg, Plaintiff-Appellee v. Scrabble Crossword Game Players, Inc.; Selchow & Righter Co.; and Crown Publishers, Defendants-Appellants, 736 F2d 485–491 (1984).

Landsberg, Plaintiff-Appellee, v. Scrabble Crossword Game Players, Inc., Selchow & Righter Co., and Crown Publishers, Inc., Defendants-Appellants, 802 F2d 1193–1200 (9th Circuit 1986).

Lawrence, Michael and John Ozag, *The Ultimate Guide to Winning Scrabble Brand Crossword Game*, Bantam Books, New York, New York, 1987.

Lemley, Mark, "The Modern Lanham Act and the Death of Common Sense," *Yale Law Journal*, vol. 108, 1685–1717, 1999.

Lemley, Mark and Eugene Volokh, "Freedom of Speech and Injunctions in Intellectual Property Cases," *Duke Law Journal*, vol. 48, 147–242, 1998.

Lunney, Glynn, Jr., "Trademark Monopolies," *Emory Law Journal*, vol. 48, 367–487, Spring 1999.

McCabe, Kathleen, "Dilution by Blurring: A Theory Caught in the Shadow of Trademark Infringement," *Fordham Law Review*, vol. 68, 1827–1875, 2000.

Miller, Wayne, *Toy Wars*, Adams Media Corporation, Holbrook, Massachusetts, 1998.

Milton Bradley Co., *The Official Scrabble Players Dictionary* (3rd Ed), East Longmeadow, Massachusetts, 1995.

Moskin, Jonathan, "Dilution or Delusion: The Rational Limits of Trademark Protection," *Trademark Review*, vol. 83, 122–148, 1993.

Mueller, Charles, "Tribute to the Human Spirit: Anti-Monopoly's 2 Decades in the U.S. Courts," *Antitrust Law and Economics Review*, vol. 29, 63–74, 1998.

National Scrabble Association, *Tournament Director's Manual*, Greenport, New York, 1999.

National Scrabble Association, *Official Tournament and Club Word List*, Merriam Webster, Springfield, Massachusetts, 1997.

National Scrabble Association, *2001 Roster of Official Scrabble Clubs of U.S. & Canada*, Greenport, New York.

National Scrabble Association, *Scrabble News*, various issues from the late 1980s to the present, Greenport, New York.

Neuberger, James, *Letter to Richard Selchow*, September 12, 1985.

Oglesby, Carole, *The Encyclopedia of Women and Sport in America*, Oryx Press, 1998.

Orleans, Jacob and Edmund Jacobson, *The Scrabble Brand Games Word Guide*, A GD/PERIGEE Book, 1953.

Pate, Jim, *Some New Terms Used in Scrabble Crossword Game Play*, Birmingham, Alabama, 2001, self published.

Person, Carl and Ralph Anspach, "FTC-Approved Monopolization in the Anti-Monopoly Case: Killing an Industry's Superstructure," *Antitrust Law & Economics Review*, vol. 25, No. 4, 81–96, 1994.

Person, Carl and Ralph Anspach, "FTC-Approved Monopolization in the Anti-Monopoly Case: Killing an Industry's Infrastructure II," *Antitrust Law & Economics Review*, vol. 26, No. 1, 99–110, 1995.

Person, Carl and Ralph Anspach, "FTC-Approved Monopolization in the Anti-Monopoly Case: Killing an Industry's Infrastructure III," *Antitrust Law & Economics Review*, vol. 26, No. 3, 67–78, 1996.

Port, Kenneth, "The Congressional Expansion of American Trademark Law: A Civil System in the Making," *Wake Forest Law Review*, vol. 35, 827–913, 2000.

Port, Kenneth, "The Unnatural Expansion of Trademark Rights: Is a Federal Dilution Statute Necessary?," *Seton Hall Legislative Journal*, vol. 18, 434–488, 1994.

Pratt, Daniel, "A Brief History of the Scrabble Players Dictionary," *Verbatim*, Winter 1999.

Reno, Doree, "The Winning Word for Scrabble Champion Is Contract," *Loyola Entertainment Law Journal*, 185–199, Winter 1988.

Scrabble Crossword Game Players Inc., *Scrabble Players Newspaper*, various issues from 1973–1986, Holbrook, New York.

Scrabble Crossword Game Players Inc., *Scrabble Symposium*, Sheraton Hotel, Boston, Massachusetts, August 1, 1985.

Selchow & Righter v. Book-of-the-Month-Club, No. 76 Civ. 462, U.S. District Court, 192 USPQ (BNA) 530, May 4, 1976.

Selchow & Righter v. McGraw-Hill Book Company, No. 77 Civ. 4505. U.S. District Court, Southern District of New York, 439 F.Supp. 243 (1977).

Selchow & Righter v. Stein and Day, U.S. District Court, Southern District of New York, Notice of Dismissal, 85 Civ. 890, May 1, 1985.

Senkiewicz, Mike, *Scrabble Players Handbook*, Selchow & Righter, 1974.

Silverman, Irwin and Krista Phillips, "The Evolutionary Psychology of Spatial Sex Differences," in Crawford, Charles and Dennis Krebs, *Handbook of Evolutionary Psychology: Ideas, Issues and Applications*, Lawrence Erlbaum Associates, Publishers, Mahwah, New Jersey, 1998.

Toho Co. v. William Morrow and Company (the Godzilla case), USPQ2d, 1801–1811, 1998.

USA Today v. New Kids on the Block, 971, Federal Reporter, 2d Series, 302–310, 1992.

Wapnick, Joel, *The Champion's Strategy for Winning at Scrabble Brand Crossword Game*, Stein and Day, 1986.

Weisfeld, Carol, "Female Behavior in Mixed-Sex Competition: A Review of the Literature," *Developmental Review*, vol. 16, 278–299, 1986.

Weisfeld, Carol and Glen Weisfeld, Ronald Warren, Daniel Freedman, "The Spelling Bee: A Naturalistic Study of Female Inhibition in Mixed-Sex Competition," *Adolescence*, vol. 28, 695–708, 1983.

Weissman, Albert and Donna Weissman, *Letters for Expert Game Players*, various issues, October 1980–December 1986, Deep River, Connecticut.